"Brilliant. Stunning. Winsome. This is ⸺⸺⸺⸺⸺ simply have to read but one you will want to return to again and again. I didn't want it to end—and now to begin living *Fiercehearted*!"

—**Ann Voskamp**, *New York Times* bestselling author of *The Broken Way* and *One Thousand Gifts*

"Fear can't catch what it can no longer reach. *Fiercehearted* will take you to new levels with the Lord as you learn to embrace the unique kind of bravery he has placed inside of you!"

—**Lysa TerKeurst**, #1 *New York Times* bestselling author and president of Proverbs 31 Ministries

"One of the things I love most about Holley is that she spends very little time in the shallows. She goes to the depths of things with God, with her friends, and with those who want to learn from her. This book is no different. Each story, every insight, reminds us we're not alone, we're loved, and we get to be works in progress. Most of us berate ourselves for our weaknesses, yet Holley's book reminds us that—because of Christ—we're stronger than we think. And though our trials are messy and our fears real, our God is with us, and he's making something out of us! Grab a cup of coffee and give yourself some time to truly ponder the wisdom on these pages. You're more *Fiercehearted* than you know."

—**Susie Larson**, talk radio host, national speaker, and author of *Your Powerful Prayers*

"This is Holley Gerth like you've never read her before. The coach and counselor are still there, but now we get to meet the warrior. Fearlessly, she opens up her childhood and her womanhood and invites us into the backstories that have shaped her. I've known Holley for nearly a decade, and this was like meeting her all over again. Her doubts and demons and her determination not to believe them. And to finally lay down who she thought she was supposed to be and receive the name God had intended for her—*Fiercehearted*.

This book is for every woman, especially those who don't believe it yet."

—**Lisa-Jo Baker**, bestselling author of *Never Unfriended* and community manager for (in)courage

"It is inevitable—we will fail and we will get hurt. We will feel afraid and we will be tempted to pull back and play it safe, but safe is nowhere near the life God calls us to! In her most vulnerable and powerful book yet, Holley Gerth lets us into the unsafe, unknown stories of her personal journey, where she is learning to love bravely, trust courageously, and live fully! Empowering us to be *Fiercehearted* in our relationships with ourselves and each other, Holley shows us how to become the women we long to be, the women God created us to be. I'm so grateful for the gift of this book, and my beautiful, brave friend Holley, who is courageously leading the way!"

—**Renee Swope**, bestselling author of *A Confident Heart*

"*Fiercehearted* is a call to arms to be our best—and most vulnerable—selves. Thank you, Holley Gerth, for writing these words. They are real and so are you."

—**Claire Diaz-Ortiz**, author and speaker

"Let's say you're in the locker room with your coach before the second half of the most important game of your life. You don't know if you can go on, but the coach's words stir something so deep inside of you that you can't wait to run back onto the court. This book is that moment, and Holley is that coach. This is what we all need to hear before we step into the rest of our lives. Don't miss this phenomenal book; it's Holley's best yet."

—**Jennifer Dukes Lee**, author of *The Happiness Dare* and *Love Idol*

"My favorite of Holley Gerth's books so far, *Fiercehearted* proves that fierce doesn't have to be intimidating, and gentle can also be brave. With the expertise of a counselor and the kindness of a friend, Holley offers permission we don't need but often wait for anyway—to be who we already are in Christ and truly live."

—**Emily P. Freeman**, author of *Simply Tuesday*

"It's rare that I open a book and the words begin to change my life on page one. *Fiercehearted* did just that. This book is honest, raw, and stunningly beautiful. It captured not only my attention but also my heart."

—**Suzanne Eller**, international speaker and author

"I didn't know how much I needed this book until I started reading it. Holley Gerth peels back facades and uncovers lies, unveiling the beautiful freedom God has for each one of us. It's time to be *Fiercehearted*!"

—**Joanna Weaver**, author of *Having a Mary Heart in a Martha World*

"Holley Gerth's words captivated my heart from the very first sentence to the all-too-soon end. *Fiercehearted* will have you crying out about your struggles, 'Me too! I'm not the only one!' Through powerfully poignant storytelling, Holley invites you to turn your broken places into brave platforms of a fiercehearted woman who risks loving, believes the impossible, and lives courageously bold."

—**Sharon Jaynes**, cofounder of Girlfriends in God, conference speaker, and author of *Take Hold of the Faith You Long For*

"Through *Fiercehearted*, Holley Gerth does what few authors do: she makes me feel at home with who I am. If you've ever felt like too much or not enough or you're in the middle of nothing special, *Fiercehearted* hand-delivers the fresh-air message that you're just right, right as you are. Holley's writing ushered me from fearhearted to fiercehearted as it helped me lean into how God made me instead of how I think I should be. I will revisit this book's pages time and again."

—**Kristen Strong**, author of *Girl Meets Change*

"In *Fiercehearted*, Holley transports us on an emotional journey by her side as she opens her heart, describing the personal relationship and strong daily focus she has with her best friend, Jesus. Her transparency and relatability throughout each story helps us realize we are on life's wonderful journey together. You will laugh and maybe even cry a little, but your faith will be strengthened with the realization that it is not perfection we each need as we persevere throughout our lives but a closeness and profound love for Jesus. Thank you, Holley, for sharing your heart through these wonderful and meaningful stories."

—**Peggy Horner**, vice president of product development for Premier Manufacturing, Inc.

fierce
HEARTED

You're Already Amazing
You're Already Amazing LifeGrowth Guide
You're Already Amazing LifeGrowth DVD
Do You Know You're Already Amazing?
You're Made for a God-Sized Dream
Opening the Door to Your God-Sized Dream
You're Going to Be Okay
What Your Heart Needs for the Hard Days
You're Loved No Matter What

fierce HEARTED

LIVE FULLY, LOVE BRAVELY

HOLLEY GERTH

Revell

a division of Baker Publishing Group
Grand Rapids, Michigan

Published by Revell
a division of Baker Publishing Group
P.O. Box 6287, Grand Rapids, MI 49516-6287
www.revellbooks.com

Printed in the United States of America

The Library of Congress Cataloging-in-Publication Data is on file at the Library of Congress, Washington, DC.

ISBN 978-0-8007-2289-0

Unless otherwise indicated, Scripture quotations are from the Holy Bible, New International Version®. NIV®. Copyright © 1973, 1978, 1984, 2011 by Biblica, Inc.™ Used by permission of Zondervan. All rights reserved worldwide. www.zondervan.com

Scripture quotations labeled KJV are from the King James Version of the Bible.

Scripture quotations labeled NASB are from the New American Standard Bible®, copyright © 1960, 1962, 1963, 1968, 1971, 1972, 1973, 1975, 1977, 1995 by The Lockman Foundation. Used by permission. All rights reserved.

Scripture quotations labeled NLT are from the Holy Bible, New Living Translation, copyright © 1996, 2004, 2015 by Tyndale House Foundation. Used by permission of Tyndale House Publishers, Inc., Carol Stream, Illinois 60188. All rights reserved.

17 18 19 20 21 22 23   7 6 5 4 3 2 1

a fierce HEARTED WOMAN . . .

looks life in the face and says, "You can't beat me."
Knows *love* is risk but reaches out anyway.
Understands *kindness* takes real courage.
BELIEVES THE IMPOSSIBLE.
Fights like she's unstoppable.
Dares to find beauty in a ragged soul.
Scandalously picks warm over cool.
Tastes life as a brief, salty-sweet miracle.
Skins her knees, has scars that bear witness.
Defends like a warrior and weeps like a girl.
Makes gentle the new strong, small the new big,
ordinary the new extraordinary.
Sees wrinkles on a face as lines in a victory story.
NEVER GIVES IN, NEVER GIVES UP, NEVER LETS GO.
Chases Jesus with a tender, world-changing wildness.
Lives in your neighborhood or not even on your continent.
Looked back at you from the mirror this morning . . .
and has yet to fully see the force her star-scattering,
mountain-moving, water-walking *God created her* TO BE.

Contents

Introduction   13

1. Unexpectedly Fiercehearted   17
2. Being Woman   22
3. Dream Machine   26
4. Scratches on the Wall   29
5. Hiding in Stalls   33
6. Swing Hard   37
7. Muddy Glory   41
8. Mango Closet   46
9. Off the Shelf   50
10. Outside the (Pink) Lines   54
11. Bone in the Chicken   59
12. Shake the Jar   63
13. Flops and Rafters   67
14. Praying Wronger   70
15. Room for Knobs   74
16. Wearing the Hat   78

CONTENTS

17. Shiny Rocks   83
18. Red Teapot   87
19. Like Water into Wine   92
20. The Ride   96
21. Crazy Sparks   100
22. Ordinary, Divine   104
23. All Favorites   108
24. Cheeky   112
25. Get a Hanky   116
26. Emotional Duct Tape   121
27. Pedicures, Mice, Therapy   126
28. Brave, Hard Thing   131
29. Different Kind of Sad   136
30. Showing Up   141
31. On Ragamuffins   145
32. Kind, Not Nice   149
33. Oh, the Audacity   154
34. Involved   158
35. Not the Only One   162
36. Hey There, Friend   167
37. Farther, Not Faster   171
38. Everyday Faithful   175
39. What I Know Now   179
40. Casseroles, Yodels, Love   184

Epilogue   189
Discussion Questions   197
Acknowledgments   201
Notes   203

Introduction

God is a storyteller. He's a mad scientist and a
father and a magician, and certainly, he's a storyteller. And I don't know if there's anything better
in the world than when we lay ourselves wide
open and let his story become our story, when
we screw up our fists and our courage and start
to tell the truest, best stories we know, which are
always God's stories.

—Shauna Niequist

I TRIED NOT TO WRITE THIS BOOK.

And before you decide to be part of it, I must warn you: there's a
bit of blood on these pages. Some sweat drips and salty tearstains,
the kind that might not come out with the washing. Laughter that
tastes like homemade vanilla ice cream churned on the patio. The
ricochet of questions against the walls. Bareness and discomfort
and beauty like a turquoise sky. There is not neatness or propriety,
proper religion or safe phrases. This is not an undertaking for the
faint of heart.

If this doesn't frighten you, if you're curious or restless or longing, then sit beside me in a coffee shop with white brick walls so I can tell you how I, how we, really got to this moment.

Ragged, beloved guitar notes flow from unseen speakers and the scent of my almond milk latte sways like a gypsy woman somewhere above us. I hear the swirl of conversations, some laced with joy and others with frustration, making the edges of the words rough. The chair I'm in is dove gray and welcomes backsides like a mama putting babies on her lap. There's a twin of this chair right across from me, and I imagine you sitting in it. You might have coffee in a chipped white mug or a teapot on a simple, elegant tray. Maybe you have a lemon scone or a blueberry muffin, and I'm hoping you'll pass me a bit of it (this is always what I'm hoping with baked goods). We talk for a while and I listen hard. Then we come to that place in the conversation where you might ask, "So what about you?"

This is the scariest question in all the universe to me. The one that makes me duck and weave like an amateur boxer in the answering. I will give you my attention all the livelong day and hardly whisper of my own life.

I thought I might like to write a book in this way. I had the title picked out and the topic selected. Yet every time I sat down to sensibly, safely write, I couldn't bring forth a word. I decided I needed to research and went to find commentaries and articles. I spent time in the library and clicking around the internet. I pulled out an impressive full-color map of Israel, complete with the Hebrew names of midnight-blue rivers and khaki mountains.

Finally, in frustration one day while sitting in this very chair, I began to simply type what was actually pulsing in my heart and ringing in my ears. I wrote about fear and brokenness. I talked about savoring life like the strange, sugary center of white honeysuckle. Fighting the doubts that sometimes wore black ski masks when they rattled my doorknobs late at night. How kindness takes courage. I told the truth about some things I'd rather keep hidden under the couch cushions with the dirty pennies. I admitted to both struggles and victories. I didn't make so many statements. I told more stories.

This felt wild and scandalous to me. Vulnerable and beautiful. Like the only thing I could birth into the world right then.

And as I began to talk with other women, I realized *I am not the only one*. I am not the only one who has ever felt unsure. I am not the only one who wants to treat today like that last glorious bite of whipped cream and chocolate pie you scrape the plate to get. I am not the only one who is looking for purpose and passion and sometimes swats depression and anxiety away like flies on a picnic table.

When you get to the end of these pages, I want you to also be able to say with certainty, "I'm not the only one." I want all of us to feel less alone and more comfortable in our God-sewn skin and a little surer that we are a force to be reckoned with in this world.

When I stepped into this book, I crossed a line. I found myself in a new place of living more fully, loving more bravely, and showing up as I really am in ways I hadn't quite dared before. This, I discovered, is the vast and wild and beautiful territory of the fiercehearted.

It is who we are, who we've been all along. Where we belong. Come with me?

Unexpectedly
fiercehearted

Truth and courage aren't always comfortable, but they're never weakness.

—Brené Brown

THE NEWS CAME ONE FALL AFTERNOON. The leaves had just started acting like that neighbor woman who always wore the plain housecoat until showing up at the block party in the audacious dress everyone talked about for weeks. Reds and oranges and flashes of gold. Perfume bittersweet as the edge of a burnt marshmallow.

I was driving to my in-laws' house when I heard the news. I wanted to push the gas pedal into the floor until it snapped and I hurtled like a loose bull down the highway. I wanted to slam the brakes so hard my tires would write my broken heart on the pavement in ugly skid marks.

I did neither. Instead, I just kept going. *Isn't that the way with us?* But inside me something invisible and fragile and essential had shattered. *Trust.* A friend had hurt me in a way I'd never expected. Normally, I'd just say, "Oh, that's okay." I tried. I gave the speech in my mind a thousand times. But it wouldn't make its way to my lips or fingertips, and I felt panicked. Because I am a woman who has always hated conflict. I would rather go under the drill at the dentist than have an argument. Yes, doctor, I'll take that root canal over exchanging tense words with someone I love. To avoid conflict I would simply try very hard to be agreeable, and when that didn't work, I'd pretend to be fine anyway. Please pass the salt and potatoes even though your fork is in my back.

Let me pause and confess I full-out know better. I have a master's degree in counseling, for goodness' sake. One of the phrases I remember most from my training is, "Conflict is the way two become one." I loved that when I heard it and thought it was quite brilliant and beautiful. But it was like loving how caviar looks all glittery and shiny at the fancy party, then realizing what's on your plate is cold and slimy and you'd rather have the cheap fish sticks the kids are eating, thanks.

I'm starting to understand there are two kinds of knowing in this world. The first is in your head, where everything makes sense and is as pristine as a laboratory. The other is the kind where Scripture says things like, "Adam *knew* Eve."[1] We used to blush and giggle in Sunday school at that one because we guessed what it *really* meant. But aside from the sexy talk, I think what that word *knew* expresses is experiencing something fully—with not only our minds but also our souls and hearts and bodies. And at the time when this hurt happened, I didn't know a thing about real, healing conflict on that kind of deeper level.

Looking back, I think I was just scared. Conflict seemed like making yourself bare and putting your whole vulnerable heart out there. I didn't appreciate the idea of my soft spots showing like a spring breaker's on the beach. And, honestly, I was afraid of what I might be capable of doing to someone else in that wary state. Better to stay buttoned up under the umbrella with my SPF 1000.

And that's actually a reasonable enough strategy until something happens and there's no backup plan. Then we're in the very place we swore we would never be, feeling all the feelings, unable to undo it.

I remembered how we're told to not let the sun go down on our anger. I'd always taken that literally, but as I thought about it more, I began to realize perhaps what that really means is not letting our anger slip into utter darkness, into bitterness and hardness.[2] I knew my only hope of that was to give my heart space to quit hissing like a terrified, trapped tomcat.

I got on a plane the day after I heard the news and stared out the window at an offensively clear evening sky as I considered my options. I wanted with every part of me, down to my boot-covered toes, to slam the door of my heart. Not just on this person but all people. I wanted to put a sign in the yard that said, "Trespassers will be shot." I wanted to board up the windows and put a mean dog on the porch. I wanted to be done with all humans everywhere for always and always.

Except I knew I still was one. And if I made this choice, I would suffocate in my own safety. Everything beautiful would become dusty. All that was alive inside would die because I couldn't let the light in. And I sensed Jesus—very kind and tender and knowing far more than I what it is to feel crucified, waiting quietly for me to decide what to do.

I pulled out something to write on and cried in the dark while the flight attendant passed out crackly packages of peanuts. I sniffled into my too-small napkin and worried about scaring my seatmate. But I couldn't stop. Because this wasn't just about this one time, this one thing. And I knew once I finished my scribbling I could never go back to who I was or how I lived before. This was my map and declaration and manifesto:

A fiercehearted woman . . .
looks life in the face and says, "You can't beat me."
Knows love is risk but reaches out anyway.
Understands kindness takes real courage.
Believes the impossible.
Fights like she's unstoppable.
Dares to find beauty in a ragged soul.
Scandalously picks warm over cool.
Tastes life as a brief, salty-sweet miracle.
Skins her knees, has scars that bear witness.
Defends like a warrior and weeps like a girl.
Makes gentle the new strong, small the new big,
ordinary the new extraordinary.
Sees wrinkles on a face as lines in a victory story.
Never gives in, never gives up, never lets go.
Chases Jesus with a tender, world-changing wildness.
Lives in your neighborhood or not even on your continent.
Looked back at you from the mirror this morning . . .
and has yet to fully see the force her star-scattering,
mountain-moving, water-walking God created her to be.

The wheels touched ground, and when we unloaded, I left some of my baggage on the plane. I left the part of me who had been nice out of fear, who had agreed because it was easier, who had silenced her own voice.

The next week I started going to counseling. The week after that I sent the person who wounded me a note. I told the truth. Of my hurt. Of my hopes for parts of our relationship becoming different. Of how much I loved her. Since then we've been making our way back toward each other again. But I'm not rushing. I'm not forcing the next step. That is both incredibly difficult and down-deep healing all at once.

I still hate conflict. But I have also come to see that it is not all "bad." That rough exterior hides gifts. Like showing us what we really want and who we really are. It threw cold water on my face and woke me up. And while I sputtered and protested at the beginning, I'm now grateful because that house I so wanted to protect was actually on fire—a slow, deceptive burn—and I didn't know it. My refusal to ever have conflict with others meant I was in conflict with myself. And every time I refused to speak the truth in love, I lit another match.

This story has no perfect, pretty ending. The relationship is still being restored, brick by slow brick, surer and stronger replacing shaky and crumbled down. The temptation to be a peacekeeper instead of a peacemaker in my everyday life is still there all the time. And I'm practicing not "getting over" things but instead walking through them—an amateur tightrope artist who wishes for wings. But I know I've made a decision to live differently. I wouldn't be here with you if it had gone the other way.

So here's to whatever brings us to the point where we can no longer stay the same. Here's to keeping the front door open. Here's to doing the brave, hard thing.

Here's to being fiercehearted.

Being
woman

Because he has spoken peace all over me, called me beautiful, Spirit-born, I fight my inner dark, choose this day the Holy.

—Amber Haines

A SINGLE RED DOT, circular and small. I sound the alarm from the tiny bathroom at the back of our house. "Mom!" She comes running at the fear and confusion in my voice. I explain, lip quivering, visions of white hospital walls and trays with green Jell-O and a funeral service already in my mind. Her face mixes smile and frown and wonder like flour and sugar and salt in a bowl. I realize then that this has something to do with a becoming. "You're a woman," she tells me.

That was decades ago, and I still don't fully understand what this phrase means. *You're a woman.* I think of other times that have brought these words into my mind. As a bride walking down the aisle on the arm of my father, whose deep breaths are the dam holding back his tears when he tucks my wrist into the tuxedo sleeve of my groom. Later that night when all that's been forbidden becomes holy and I am naked and unashamed. When I am on the table of a doctor with an ultrasound wand in her hand and she is looking at the quiet screen and telling us, "I'm sorry."

Didn't all this spill out from that single drop, a red sea without the parting? And there's more to being a woman than just these events. Something in my girl bones knows this as I watch the mamas and grandmas, the big sisters and aunties, the single adventurers and the seniors with their coveted casserole dishes on Sundays. I want to know what it means to be a woman on the inside, too, in the places where the shouts come from and the river of tears begins and the laughter rolls out like thunder.

I go hunting in Genesis for answers because it is the beginning of all things:

> But for Adam no suitable helper was found. So the LORD God caused the man to fall into a deep sleep; and while he was sleeping, he took one of the man's ribs and then closed up the place with flesh. Then the LORD God made a woman from the rib he had taken out of the man, and he brought her to the man. (Gen. 2:21–22)

People who mean well use these words to build definitions and limits and expectations around femininity like fences. And it will be too many years before I read what Sharon Jaynes says in *How Jesus Broke the Rules to Set You Free,* when I begin to really understand.

> The Hebrew word "helper" that is used for woman is *ezer*. It is derived from the Hebrew word used of God and the Holy Spirit, "azar." Both mean "helper"—one who comes alongside to aid or assist. King David wrote, "O LORD, be my helper" (Ps. 30:10 NASB). . . .
>
> Ezer appears twenty-one times in the Old Testament. Two times it is used of the woman in Genesis 2, sixteen times it is used of

God or Yahweh as the helper of his people. The remaining three references appear in the books of the prophets, who use it in reference to military aid.[1]

When I discover this, it's like a sledgehammer to a stained glass window. Shards and color and the only perspective I could see for so long are sent flying in every direction. And all these pieces settle into something new, a mosaic of beauty and mystery and wildness I did not know I was allowed.

We are women and this is a powerful thing. It is an echo of God's heart and a display of his glory. He speaks this world into being—*let there be light*—but when he makes woman, it's intimate, and personal.

Imagine the scene. Adam drifting off to sleep in the sunlight, the whisper of God's footsteps on the grass, the bend of his knees as he reaches down. He touches Adam's side, the place closest to his heart, and takes hold of a rib. Perhaps the animals gather to watch. A porcupine with sharp quills who's trying not to be socially awkward sits next to a chubby panda having another afternoon snack, while a squirrel deliriously runs circles around them all. Then a hush comes as the Artist begins to work. He stretches the rib out long and adds curves and flesh and eyelashes. Yes, a freckle just above her lip, a wrinkle on her elbow, a softness in the palms of her hands, and a strength between her shoulder blades.

I think God smiles.

Soon all that beauty will be marred with sin like spitballs on the ceiling of the Sistine Chapel. He will curse her. He will not give up on her. And later a Messiah will set her free. But even after that the woman circles the borders of Eden, never completely reclaiming the truth. She forgets her story. The people around her tell her different versions. The world is a web of lies and she is the butterfly with paper wings struggling in the corner.

She doesn't see she is lovely. She becomes untethered from the fierceness inside her. She tries on shoes like Cinderella in yoga pants and eats leftover cookies alone in the middle of the night and sees the plastic surgeon for one more touch-up, the knife splitting her skin's surface like the hurt splits her soul. Or she hides and tries very hard to be very good. She joins every committee and says yes to bathing one hundred poodles for charity and grows dim in the flicker of the television light.

And all the while, the One who made her is calling her back, still walking in the garden of her heart in the cool of the day and saying, "I am with you." He offers what she longs for most—for him to tell her who she really is, to whisper in her ear that he has made her funny and wise and strong and brave. That she is tender and resilient and complex and wonder-filled. She is mystery and unveiling. She is salty tears and the sweat at the finish line and the lioness in the corner office and lullabies in the night. She is not an afterthought; she has been an essential part of the plan all along.

Somewhere a snake hisses and a Savior on a cross declares, "It is finished." A single red drop falls to the ground. The curtain splits and the curse breaks and the promise of Eden comes back to us. All the sisters and the daughters and the mamas say, "Amen." Redemption joyfully roars back, "You are a woman." And it echoes through the ages all the way down to a tiny bathroom in the back of a house.

When I listen closely, I can hear it still.

Let's be
women
who know
we are not **eye candy**
but works of art,
not stereotypes
but **STRONG** forces,
not role-players
but world
SHAPERS.

dream Machine

> Tell me, what is it you plan to do with your one wild and precious life?
>
> —Mary Oliver

IN TEXAS, the summers stretch as long and lazy as hounds. If you are a child in such a place, then your only hope is to stay submerged in some type of water for as much time as possible or find a diversion entertaining enough to distract you out of heatstroke.

One blazing afternoon my best friend pounded on our back door and described finding a treasure at a garage sale worth pooling all our allowance money to purchase. So we hopped on our bikes and went back to the scene of the discovery. And there it sat in all its glory. An old paddleboat the color of bright yellow margarine, its underside retrofitted with wheels so it could be driven on land through the use of two sets of pedals. We bought it immediately.

My mom surveyed our purchase and insisted we add an orange safety flag. It waved above us at the top of a white stick as we set out like a sherbet circus. The wheels were wider than the sidewalk, but we were forbidden to drive on the road. So we straddled concrete strips in front of unsuspecting suburban houses and left skid marks in the grass. When we tired of touring, we decided to retreat to my friend's street, a cul-de-sac with a house being built at the end of it. Our Dream Machine (yes, we named it) became an all-terrain vehicle as we made circles in the mud and then pedaled down the new cement driveway at NASCAR-ish speeds.

Such a spectacle could not go unnoticed. Before long, children of all shapes, sizes, and ages began to peer out of windows and step outside doors. Our appropriately colored paddleboat became a taxi, and we offered rides to any willing passenger. As I recall, at one moment we had five kids piled on the back. Hair flying in the wind, shirts sticking to shoulders with a mix of sweat and fear-laced adrenaline, the stain of popsicles still on our fingers. We owned the world.

And then without warning or explanation, the steering wheel fell off. We slowed to a halt, debarked, and stared at the former glory of the Dream Machine with sighs and head scratching. I'm sure someone's mother hollered for them to come home and someone else had a *Gilligan's Island* rerun to watch and another kid got hungry. My friend and I found ourselves alone with the wreckage of that unexpected summer wonder. The details fade out of focus here, but the two of us must have dragged it out of the cul-de-sac and into the corner of a garage or backyard.

It's funny, I don't remember feeling regret about how we treated that poor paddleboat. We never thought, *Maybe we shouldn't have enjoyed ourselves quite so much*. We didn't say, "We really shouldn't have shared it with anyone." We knew better than I seem to know now that nothing in this world lasts forever. We are dust and our lives have all the lovely brevity of "wildflowers" (Ps. 103:15 NLT). At some moment the steering wheel always comes off and the ride is over.

I've lost several dreams in the last decade. Things in my life I cherished and chose and took to with the wide-eyed wonder of a child on the pony she never expected to get for Christmas. And when I think about those dreams, I sometimes feel the way I did in the street the day the steering wheel fell off. A little sad, confused, and unsure of what to do next.

Part of me wants to climb into the front seat again and stay there until time impossibly turns back. Part of me wants to figure out how to fix the problem. Part of me wants to get very spiritual and explain it all away. But those are the grown-up parts of me. The wiser, younger part inside knows we all must face moments of letting go. When something turns out to be temporary, the time we had with it isn't worthless; it's precious and irreplaceable.

My friend and I went on to have other adventures. We played hide-and-seek. Occasionally terrorized teenage lifeguards wearing smirks and silver whistles. Captured dozens of baby turtles from prohibited golf course ponds and treated them like rare green jewels that just happened to eat wilted lettuce and leftover ham. The summer slipped into fall, school resumed, and life went on. Because that's what life does.

I don't know what happened to the Dream Machine. I hope somehow another pair of kids got hold of it and turned it into a pirate fort or a slightly smelly sandbox or a makeshift bed for a dog with freckles on its nose. For me, it will always be a soul signpost from my childhood. A reminder of being reckless and present in the best ways. Something odd and lovely and true, a yellow margarine memory whispering in my ear, "It's a brave thing to stay fully alive in all your living."

scratches
on the Wall

To believe in yourself means to believe that God made you and there is no one like you, that you have a unique call to courage, and that you can do the thing that is staring you in the face.

—Annie Downs

MY FAVORITE CAFÉ is crowded this morning. I navigate tables occupied by friends deep in conversation, business folks with papers spread out, students burying their heads in thick, battered textbooks. I finally wedge myself into a seat at a counter. I notice a few names subtly scratched into the old brick wall I'm facing. *Don't we all live a bit like small-time graffiti artists?*

We're desperate to etch into the surface of history something that proves we were here. Perhaps this is on my mind because I'm feeling unseen and a bit lost. Small and uncertain in ways I haven't for a long while.

Today feels different because I don't quite know my way out of these emotions. Normally, I'd just outrun them. For years the folks who know me best would have called me "driven." I always had the map out, a destination in mind. Always pushing, pushing, pushing. Gas pedal to the floor. No time for bathroom breaks or snapping pictures of that extraordinary view. No, I needed to *arrive*.

And in some ways I did. I put neat little checkmarks by several of the places I wanted to go in this life. But instead of being totally satisfied, I sometimes felt like tourists tend to when they finally see the Statue of Liberty or the Hollywood Walk of Fame or Mount Rushmore. "Sure, it's great," they say. "But it's not all I imagined." That's the dark alley behind hope-turned-reality or "success" that no one talks about much. Finding yourself in a space of unexpected disappointment can seem dishonorable at best and downright ungrateful at worst. Yet if I'm truthful, I've occasionally woken up there, startled and confused, surrounded by newlyweds still tan from beach honeymoons and corporate ladder climbers who just got promotions and sleep-deprived mothers with spit-up on their shoulders.

Sometimes I miss the season of chasing, imagining, pursuing, and glimpsing. Because that's when the vision is all you have. *And the vision is perfect*. It doesn't have lonely moments. It doesn't come with discouragement or laundry or critics. It doesn't ever remind you of the enticing cheesecake on the dessert tray that wound up suspiciously tasting a bit like it may have come from a cardboard package.

And when a dream that becomes reality doesn't fully satisfy, it makes future dreaming harder because we don't believe as innocently as before that a pot of gold (or happiness or fulfillment or the cure-all for our insecurities) is waiting at the end of the rainbow. The noble reasons we gave for all our goals are no longer so shiny either. We realize that even though, yes, our efforts were to honor God and help other people, it sure was about us too. We had expectations. We had demands. We bet all our money on that horse.

This can be a bit unnerving, especially when we've never had a backup plan. All my life, I've only ever thought of being a writer.

The granddaughter of a bookstore owner, I felt books were my home and calling and friends. I don't remember a time when I didn't love words. I can't recall a moment when pages weren't the best mirror and magnifying glass in my world. And I thought when I "made it," when I saw my titles on shelves and heard people say, "What you wrote changed my life," then I would somehow be whole.

My husband and I took a walk last night under a brilliantly blue, early spring sky. Our fourteen-year-old beagle-basset mix trotted in front of us, nose to the ground. We talked about how I'm taking a bit of a sabbatical from speaking engagements, because as much as I want to love events with large groups, they can drain me dry as a desert. It can take weeks for me to recover. In the middle of our conversation, tears came to my eyes and I said, "I thought if I could just be successful enough, I would become someone else. But you can't grow into someone new. You can only grow into more of *you*."

I really did believe that if I just tried hard enough, I could become a more outgoing, popular kind of person. I thought I would stop being an introvert. I thought I would quit loving a quiet house more than a loud party. I thought I would learn to make small talk and maybe, just maybe, even manage to be a tiny bit cool. But success doesn't change us; it only magnifies who we truly are.

I'm not looking for pity or compliments—I know I have strengths, gifts, and talents too. But I've wrestled with parts of who I am like rogue alligators ever since I stepped into a school lunchroom and realized I might not ever have a seat at *that* table.

Yet in moments like the ones last night with my husband, I feel as if I'm not in a lunchroom but on the welcome mat outside a different type of door. If I make up my mind to accept who I am once and for all, I can push that door open and I will love the life I have so much more than before.

But to be flat-out honest, my heart isn't there this morning. I'm still standing on the porch grieving because it feels like I've held an alternate version of myself inside my mind for as long as I can remember. And that person has recently died. Or, more accurately, like with Santa, the tooth fairy, and all other cherished childhood fantasies, I've come to the appalling realization she never existed. Yet it still feels like crossing the threshold of that door would mean leaving her behind forever. I would miss her.

This "other" me is talkative and never awkward in social situations. She's completely at home on a stage and holds a microphone like her beloved firstborn child. She hosts dinner parties where people laugh late into the evening on her patio beneath strings of twinkle lights. She does exciting things in exotic places and doesn't kill every plant she's ever owned. If she wrote my name on the café wall, it would be in bubble letters and the "o" would be a perfectly round circle (or maybe even a heart).

Jesus said we all must deny ourselves, and perhaps this is part of what he meant. That at some point in our lives, we must give up trying to become someone he never intended us to be. We must surrender our big illusions and egos. We must discover that we are small and ordinary—and both are really quite wonderful.

These are the lessons I'm learning, and I don't like them. But I can feel in them the promise of new freedom. Even joy.

The imaginary version of me might be bold enough to scratch my name into the brick wall of the café this morning before I go. But maybe the bravest thing is deciding we don't need to prove we were here. Maybe real courage is simply bearing witness to the wild and mysterious story God has always been writing. Perhaps true success is finally believing our actual, everyday part in his story is good . . . *and good enough.*

P.S. Time has passed and it turns out getting deep-down honest with God, myself, and others about all this was the step that finally propelled me across the threshold of that door into more of who I really am.

And—surprise!—I don't miss the other "me" at all.

Not even a smidgen.

hiding
in Stalls

God had made me this way on purpose. My way of
being was not a defect, a weakness, or something
we just had to learn to work around. It was, instead,
a strength . . . I had to learn to accept and welcome
my own true self.

—Kay Bruner

THE BATHROOM STALLS in my elementary school had
practical, cream-colored walls and doors. Grayish-white speck-
led squares of tile. Shiny silver bolts that slid delightfully and
satisfyingly into place. I'd often stand inside those little boxes
not for the usual purposes but for a few moments of quiet. *In-
out-in-out-in-out* I'd watch my chest go until the rhythm slowed.

I also knew the kind school nurse and her office well. Perhaps
sensing the true nature of my complaints, she'd escort me to a
small room in the back that smelled like bubble gum and cartoon-
covered Band-Aids. Once there, I could lie down on a comforting

little bed with a welcoming blue mattress. I'd stare at a spot on the ceiling and imagine traveling through a tunnel to a secret cave containing my very own fish tank, apparently the best and most exotic fantasy I could come up with at the age of five.

My concerned parents became perplexed about the frequent tummy aches I complained of when I came home. They took me from doctor to doctor and sat with me through test after test, but no physical ailment could be found. The answer finally and vaguely given with a shrug of shoulders was simply "stress."

It would not be until college that I would begin to see the fuller picture. I remember sitting cross-legged on the worn gray carpet of a campus ministry building and hearing the word *introvert* for the first time. I realized, with a rush of shock and relief, *I'm not the only one*.

Susan Cain, author of *Quiet*, describes my tribe this way:

> Introverts . . . may have strong social skills and enjoy parties and business meetings, but after a while wish they were home in their pajamas. They prefer to devote their social energies to close friends, colleagues, and family. They listen more than they talk, think before they speak, and often feel as if they express themselves better in writing than in conversation. They tend to dislike conflict. Many have a horror of small talk, but enjoy deep discussions.[1]

Lots of introverts (like me) also have highly sensitive nervous systems.[2] I often explain it this way. Our nervous systems are always active. They work a bit like fisherwomen's nets to capture what's going on in and around us. Some of our nets have big holes, but the sensitive sort have tiny holes. This means sensitive nets catch everything—the smallest nuances in expressions or emotions, all the words in the a-bit-too-loud music in the restaurant, the un-spoken dynamics of every relationship in the group. And because of this, nets like mine get full quite quickly.

In a chaotic elementary school classroom, there was just too much coming at me. At some point I needed silence and solitude for my nervous system to process all that stimulation (aka "empty my net") before I could comfortably take in more.

Lest you think I spent my childhood in hiding, I do have other recollections of those years. I always had my own beloved, slightly mischievous tribe of dear friends (and still do today). I recall writing brightly colored notes describing what I liked most about each of them and frequently sneaking such tributes into desks or lockers, much to their delight. I remember riding my bike along a winding path as the sun threw its final flames at the horizon and feeling like Jesus was right there with me. I still look back with affection (and a bit of envy) on the days when I had a backside small enough to nestle into the fork between two tree branches as if I were a contented blond-feathered bird, the book in my hands my wings.

These memories are not separate from the bathroom stall and the school nurse's office. They are two ends of the same stick. My introversion and sensitive nervous system contributed to uncomfortable moments and anxiety. But they also gave me empathy and creativity.

Maybe you have different sorts of memories. You might have been the child sent to time-out for talking endlessly. Perhaps you sometimes bit your tongue until it stung because you wanted so badly to say *one more thing*. While the world seemed to be whispering "you're not quite enough" into my ears, you might have felt like you heard "you're just a bit too much."

We all experience moments when we're tempted to listen to those accusations, to divide who we are into what's "good" versus "bad." But, really, there is only being human. And this means we are shifting kaleidoscopes of strangeness and brilliance, weakness and strength, courage and fear, glory and falling, one-of-a-kind and a-lot-like-everyone-else.

If I could go back to my elementary school, I'd walk into the bathroom and knock on the stall with the untied, grass-stained sneakers underneath. After the silver lock slid open, I'd look into that girl's eyes and say, "You're going to be okay. *Actually, you're going to be quite wonderful.* So never give anyone or anything the power to shame you. You're braver than you feel, stronger than you know, and loved more than you've yet to see."

Then I'd close that cream-colored door and let her be.

swing Hard

> Brave is a whisper some days and others it's a battle cry.
>
> —Lisa-Jo Baker

I'M ANGRY THIS MORNING. White-hot mad. And this is an emotion that doesn't come easily for me. I'll pick hurt over hollering or down-and-dirty fighting in almost any circumstance.

You read that right—I did say *almost*. If you're feeling brave, settle in and I'll tell you the exceptions.

My little ring of elementary school friends (including the co-owner of the Dream Machine) spent hours at "the swing." Before you imagine innocent plastic seats attached to sturdy metal chains, let me explain.

The swing was actually a long, slightly frayed rope hung from the very highest branch of the very tallest tree. It dangled over a steep embankment covered in red Texas dirt with roots running through it like pythons. An exceptionally adventurous family created the swing before the days when everyone sued everyone for everything. They welcomed any wandering child to use it—unsupervised. Oh, what unlitigated bliss.

At the top of the slope, where the swing beckoned enticingly, were splinter-infested stairs leading to a shaky wooden platform. This set-up certainly violated every building code known to human-kind. The idea was to grab the knot at the end of the rope, climb the aforementioned stairs, then jump off and swing (hence the name) over the open expanse as far as possible.

One day my hands, slick with sweat and quite possibly leftover ice cream, slid right off the rope. I dropped several feet before I landed with all the grace of a drunken monkey. Normally, I tried to put on a no-pain, no-gain face during my tomboy undertakings. But on this occasion, I howled for my mama so loudly someone swiftly fetched her.

The only other time I recall tears at the swing involved a bully from my school. Square-shouldered and dark-headed, he would sometimes show up uninvited to pick on us for crimes like having glasses or eating too much candy or, in my case, being a girl. Stand-ing on that rock-dotted incline, he glared at me and called me a word none of us were supposed to utter under any circumstance. A word particularly unkind to those of my gender. I asked him to stop. Instead, he just turned up the volume and added a slight shove for emphasis.

And that was quite enough, thank you very much.

I twisted his arm, spun him around, and wrestled him to the rust-colored ground. Then I sat right on top of him like a stunned, sprawled-out horse. Once he caught his breath, I calmly requested an apology. After a few seconds of considering his predicament, he reluctantly muttered one. So I let him up, dusted off my acid-washed jean shorts, and started to get in line for my next turn on the swing.

But his repentance was fleeting, and as I walked away I heard the same ugly word. So I repeated my amateur cowgirl-meets-ninja act. Perched once again on his still-defiant back, I felt absolutely exasperated. Why didn't he understand this wasn't going to turn out well no matter how many times he tried it? Because of his stubbornness, I had the unfortunate burden of defending the reputation of all women everywhere yet again (because I certainly considered myself an appointed agent of global justice in that moment).

I don't think I ever actually hurt anything but that bully's pride. But being tackled by a girl proved too humiliating, so he finally relented. After that day he left us alone. And years later we all went swimming in his backyard pool like nothing ever happened.

This morning I'm angry because my life has been feeling a lot like that showdown at the swing. I've recently been battling anxiety again, which always comes with lies and accusations from the enemy of my soul. He hurls the most vicious words at me during my most vulnerable moments. I know he can't beat me, but sometimes I just get downright frustrated with fighting someone who is going to lose. Every. Single. Time. It's exhausting. I just want to get back to important things, the grown-up versions of swings and friends and going home to eat watermelon on the back porch with sticky hands while spitting seeds in impressive arcs toward the yard. There is only so much time in the day, after all.

Perhaps if this battle were mine alone I might just let the bully keep on shoutin'. But I don't believe this battle is only about me. It's about all my sisters. It's about all my daughters. It's about every woman in this world. Because every time one of us wins, we all do. We silence the roar of darkness a little more. We make it a bit harder for that bully to try something on one of us again.

A fool-headed boy messed with the wrong sweet girl that day at the swing. When I finally let him up for good, my friends looked at me with eyes round as our bike tires. I think they were both shocked and downright thrilled that the often quiet, typically gentle one took down the bully. News flash: I haven't stopped.

And I hope you won't either. We will all have days when we're white-hot mad we have to go another round. We will all have moments when we want to run right on home. We will all have seasons when it seems easier just to take it. But that isn't our destiny. We are tree-swingers and baby-rockers and mountain-movers. We are girls. We are *women*. We are daughters of Eve in a fallen world. This means we will never stop being under attack. But it also means we will never—*Dear Jesus, may we never*—stop fighting back.

LET'S BE **unexpected** WARRIORS,
love ninjas, secret agents of *grace*
in the kitchens and the boardrooms
and by the *swings* on the playground.
THEY'LL NEVER SEE *us* COMING.

Muddy
glory

I believe he's created us wild—with beautiful, full, abundant, different identities. And I believe that he created us—women, his daughters, as good and as in his image. I think the more we look at him, the more we learn about ourselves, the more we're able to take a deep breath and walk in the wild identity he's given us.

—Jess Connolly

YESTERDAY AFTERNOON the sky cracked wide and white thunderhead clouds spilled rain until miniature rivers ran down the streets. I tentatively ventured out to meet a friend during a small break in the downpour. I made sure to take my umbrella. I wanted my sturdiest shoes. I worried a bit about my hair in the humidity. Then as I drove through my neighborhood, I noticed two little girls, one in bright pink and the other in lemonade yellow, jumping in puddles with looks of bliss on their faces. They waved as I went by, clearly considering themselves the luckier of us—them wet and me dry.

And I thought back to similar times in my own childhood. My little friends and I would fling open the doors after a storm like captives set free from the monotony of watching the world go by outside our windows. We would slip off our shoes (if we had any on in the first place) and take to the yard or streets. We'd find small circles of water and jump in or splash each other, exuberant and soaked. By the time we returned home, we'd be mud-speckled and spent, searching the kitchen for a snack and desperately in need of a bath.

I have been thinking lately about what childlike faith really means. For so long I pictured it as clean, cherub-like faces staring intently and sweetly at their Father without making a single sound. But I have many friends who have small children, and they do not act like this. And when I was a child, I didn't either.

My sweet mama worked as an occupational therapist for more than thirty years. Most of her clients were kids three to six years old. The therapy she did with them was based on play—using hands and arms and feet and imaginations. She encouraged my younger brother and I to play at home too. And not to just do so quietly and in a corner. She wanted us to dig in the dirt of the garden. To catch ladybugs and fat, croaking frogs. To pile bubbles up in the tub until they slopped right over the sides.

At night when she tucked us in, she would tell us stories of her own making. One I asked for over and over was about Dainty doodlebug (doodlebug is a synonym for roly poly—a small, gray bug that curls into a little protective ball when threatened). In this epic tale, Dainty is a prissy little thing who refuses to roll up like her peers. It went like this:

Under a flower bush lived a family of doodle bugs. Mama, Papa, and their daughter, Dainty. All the doodlebugs in the garden liked to get together. They would roll and roll until dust filled the air.

But Dainty never joined in. Instead, she spent her time look-ing at her reflection in the little drops of dew that landed on the flowers. Dainty did not like dirt. She did not like dust. She did not like messing up her eyelashes.

"Dainty," her mama would say, "you need to practice roll-ing up into a ball!" Dainty would pretend not to hear. Then she would make another pair of shoes from the flower petals. She needed one hundred for all her feet.

On Dainty's birthday, her family threw a big party for the whole neighborhood. Everyone brought treats. A blueberry from the garden. An acorn from the oak tree. And Dainty's favorite, rose petal tea.

Just as everyone sat down at the twiggy table, a shadow ap-peared overhead. "Bird!" everyone yelled. They had practiced many times and all knew what to do. But Dainty had been making shoes!

Everyone rolled up into little balls and disappeared under the twiggy table. But Dainty just sat there looking at the sky. The bird was so big! She was so scared!

"Roll up, Dainty!" everyone began to yell. Dainty thought about her eyelashes. She thought about her pink bow. She thought about her flower petal shoes. She thought about how she did not like dirt. She did not like dust. She did not want to be like the other silly doodlebugs.

The shadow came closer.

"But I also do not want to be eaten by a bird!" thought Dainty. Then she panicked. How did she even roll into a ball? She didn't know!

"You can do it, Dainty!" said her papa.

"You can do it, Dainty!" said her mama.

"You can do it, Dainty!" said all her friends.

And you know what? Dainty did! She rolled into a ball just as if she'd done it every day of her life. She rolled right under the twiggy table and there, safe with her friends and family, they all watched the bird fly up, up, up into the blue sky.

It was quiet for a moment. Then everyone cheered. "You did it, Dainty!" they all said, "We knew you could!"

Dainty smiled so wide. She smiled wider than when she brushed her eyelashes. She smiled wider than when she put on a pink bow. She smiled wider than when she finished a pair of shoes.

Then she said something no one ever expected, "I like dirt!"

Everyone laughed and laughed. Then they all hugged her. And from that day on, Dainty could be found with all the other doodle bugs in the garden. She put on her pink flower shoes and rolled and rolled and rolled.

Moral of the story: Don't be afraid to get messy; it just might save your life.

And in my household, that held true. We never got in trouble for coming home with wet clothes from running through sprinklers or grass stains on our knees or smelling like a locker room after playing tackle football for hours. We were allowed to carry home animals of all shapes and kinds, which we frequently did, including a surprising assortment of feisty turtles and white-bellied baby catfish in murky buckets. We had shaving cream fights in the backyard, shot silly string at each other in epic battles, and launched water balloons like grenades.

All this came back to me as I watched those two little girls dance in puddles after the storm. In that instant, I realized that childlike faith is probably far messier than I have thought it to be. Children are drawn to the dirt like little magnets. They're not afraid to touch it, to dig fingers in deep, to have it splatter all over them. They're not so preoccupied with keeping themselves clean that they miss the experience and the wonder. What if we lived that way too? Not holding back from the disarray of life and relationships but instead diving right into the middle of it all.

Children also lack our grown-up self-consciousness. There is no "I" when they're fully engaged in play with each another. There's only the enthusiastic and rowdy "we." No insecurity. No second-guessing. No wondering what anyone thinks. Just reckless abandon to the moment and the magic of whatever is in front of them. This leads to a particular kind of fearlessness—climbing fences and racing bikes and chasing the wagging tail of that dog. There is no procrastination or calculation. No endlessly analyzing the situation to make sure everything is in place and nothing could possibly go wrong. And, of course, there is *joy*. Delight in the bouquet of weeds. Dripping popsicles. Wrestling and resting, backs flat in the grass.

Along the way our grown-up selves just become a little forgetful. We tell ourselves God doesn't want carefree children but perpetually responsible adults. So we need to sit up straight and pay attention. We need to stop asking questions and start following orders. We need to settle down and try not to be so curious or wild. "But Jesus said, 'Let the children come to me. Don't stop them! For the Kingdom of heaven belongs to those who are like these children'" (Matt. 19:14 NLT).

Maybe what God really wants are grown-up kids who dance in the puddles, who aren't afraid to get their hands dirty, who dare to ask why a whole lot. Maybe we are far too proper. Maybe it's time to take a page from Dainty doodlebug's story and give in to the way we're created to live—for our sake and for the gospel. Little else is as compelling and glorious as a giddy child, mud-covered and grinning, because they know how loved and safe they are even while thunder sounds in the distance.

mango
Closet

SOME PEOPLE ENJOY A NICE PEDESTAL. Perch them atop one and they'll survey the scene, clear their throats, and proceed with changing the world. They seem immune to the expectations and risks such a height inherently brings.

I am not such a person.

After years of being a youth group leader and trying quite hard to be perfect, I knew exactly what I wanted to do with the pedestal I'd been given: chainsaw that sucker into sawdust. The edge of my blade came in the form of attending a college ten hours away from home, where no one could keep an eye on me. Almost as soon as I stepped onto campus I pulled the start cord, revved the motor by

46

uncharacteristically joining a sorority, and toppled the towering list of rules I'd sworn to follow.

With that task complete, I began to pay closer attention to the "freedom" I thought would take my pedestal's place. I imagined this freedom would taste like the artificially red punch served up by winking boys at fraternity houses. I believed it would smell like a hint of cigarettes lingering in the air even after the party was over. I assumed it would sound like the voices of new friends welcoming me with affectionate, slightly slurred words. I was certain it would look and feel like me finally doing exactly what I wanted to without conscience or consequence.

But it didn't.

I was the freshman cliché—the good girl gone at least a bit bad. And I hated it. I cried into sticky plastic cups and alone in the shower and on the unfortunate shoulder of anyone who would listen. I went home at Christmas break utterly broken. When I dared to pray, I told God, "I miss you. I don't want to keep living like this. But I can't go back to the way things were before."

One day in the new semester after Christmas break, a woman on the staff of a campus ministry struck up a conversation with me. We began spending time together and she told me about a "summer project" for college kids from around the country. I could spend three months living a few hours from campus in a neighboring state. Desperate for something new in my life, I decided to go.

On the first day, I showed up at a two-story, weatherworn former hotel converted into housing for several dozen of us. I shared a room with two other girls and we named our space the "mango closet" in honor of its size and outrageous color. We didn't have air-conditioning and, as I recall, our showerhead was akin to a green garden hose sticking out of the wall like a one-eyed snake. And still, we were smitten.

Everyone had jobs in the community—I attempted to be a waitress at a steakhouse. I was terrible at greeting strangers and at money math. One day my cash didn't balance and I actually paid the restaurant for the privilege of being there for eight hours.

When we weren't working, all the summer project students went rock climbing and square-danced in the house's living room. We floated in boats on the river and dove into the ice-cold water on hot-enough-to-fry-an-egg-on-the-deck days. We ran like whooping banshees through the woods and did battle on miniature golf courses. We blushed over unconfessed crushes and drank far too much Kool-Aid. We talked for hours about nothing and everything.

I truly don't remember the Bible studies we did that summer or any official church services—although I know both were part of the rhythm of our time too. The experiences that happened outside of those familiar things turned out to be what changed me most. Because, in the middle of the laughter and the mess and the innocent adventures, I discovered something entirely unexpected and holy: *grace*.

I tasted it in salty hot dogs on slightly stale buns eaten at picnic tables and served with a side of soul-honest stories. I smelled it in the marshmallow-laced whiff of a nearby campfire as I stared up at the faraway stars and thought in a new way about their Maker. I heard it in the endless smacks of so many flip-flops up and down stairs as we figured out a bit of what living in weird, sweet community might really mean. I saw and felt it in the grown-ups who freely, crazily gave up their peaceful, comfortable lives to invest in us.

I spent three years in the white sorority house and only three months in the mango closet. But the latter altered me most. I recently went back to the spot where that old hotel used to be. It's a Starbucks now, with cars winding around the building and folks lined up at the counter, each hoping for just a little something to make life better. I wondered where they came from and where they would go with their tall vanilla lattes and venti iced mochas (hold the whipped cream).

Kaitlyn Bouchillon says, "We live in the tension of the Already and the Not Yet. I have been redeemed; I am being redeemed. I am made new; I am being made new. We belong to the Kingdom but for now, we are all just walking each other home."[1]

Heaven is home, and we are all just wanderers this side of it. I'm so glad the winding path of my life passed through that summer project with those grace people. No pedestals present. Only ordinary, feet-on-the-ground folks figuring life out together. Maybe humble, holy ground is the only vantage point where we can really see each other, where we just might proceed to change the world.

Off the
shelf

I'M IN THE LIBRARY THIS MORNING. After writing at coffee shops so often, I've forgotten how much I love this place. How the quiet spreads out like white frosting interrupted only by a few giggles scattered like confetti-colored sprinkles from the children's section. Behind me are seemingly endless shelves of books. Love and war, mysteries and memoirs, one about a girl dragonfly with wings of flame. At this very moment, I could stand up, take a few steps, and choose any of them.

Yesterday my counselor and I talked about how life can feel this way as well. It seems there are thousands of stories we could be living. And in this world of option and opportunity we believe we could somehow pick any or all of them. We call this freedom, yet in so many ways it can become a trap. Because instead of living fully in the reality I've been given, I'm often somewhere else, lost on the pages of "what might have been" or "what could be." I want someone else's story—a book with a more enticing cover.

Years ago I went to a conference and on the first night there was a speaker dinner. Someone who lived in town offered up their backyard for the occasion, and it was simply lovely. A long, wooden picnic table with wildflowers in mason jars. Chandeliers made from twisted vines dangling above us. And into that scene, just a few minutes late, walked a woman who could have been the princess of this (or any) fairy tale–ish scene. Long blond hair, flowy dress, brilliant smile. I'd already been feeling out of place and instantly thought, *If only I could be her.*

The next day I sat in on her session for the conference, and a few minutes into her talk she pulled a circle of white cotton from her purse. She dabbed make-up remover on it and as she talked, she wiped, bit by bit, all the pink lipstick and creamy foundation and sunset blush right off her gorgeous face. She stood there bare and told us, "Behind the beautiful there is always brokenness." Then she told us of a heartbreak in her life she'd never spoken of out loud in public before. Hurt and betrayal, pain and wondering, soul-shattering moments. I never would have guessed.

And I thought of a girl I once knew who looked so much like a younger version of this woman standing before me. Voted best-liked in our eighth-grade class. Always wearing the latest pair of jeans. Asked out by the cutest boys. I followed the plotline of her existence from afar and sometimes wished I could trade mine for hers because everything in her world seemed so perfect. Then one day when we were both in high school, her daddy took his own life. I came home to my ordinary house and no-name-brand clothes feeling so sad for her and realizing we just don't know, we just don't know at all.

So often when we look at each other's lives it's like seeing only the cover of a book or maybe the little blurb of highlights on the back. But we don't know in chapter seven the tornado ripped through the roof and she's still wandering around on the lawn collecting splinters of picture frames. We don't understand in chapter three she was the kid with rubber-banded braces on her teeth, volcanoes of pimples on her face, and more pounds than she wanted around her middle. And that's who she still sees every time she looks in the mirror. We don't grasp that there is no Wizard of Oz, and behind the curtain she's just as scared and small as the rest of us.

I am at a place in my life when I want to stop constantly scanning the shelves for something on-the-surface better. Something thrilling and adventurous. Something a little more wise or funny. Something shinier than what I've been given. Instead, I want to realize that while the details are different, in so many ways our stories are the same. They are all full of anger and fear, struggle and loss, hope and longing.

And I want to be a little more open about my story, which is why I've written this book. Because maybe someone is looking at me the way I've looked at folks whose stories seem better than mine, like the woman at the conference or my school classmate. Maybe someone sees you that way too.

I hope we can find the courage to stand beside each other, point to the pages, and say, "This is the paragraph I wish I could mark out with a wide, red pen. This is the ugly, unwelcome sentence. This is the black-as-night period I was so hoping would only be a tiny, gray comma. This is the part about the hurt and the doubt following me like a stray dog. Here's where the cherry pie got thrown against the wall and, yes, the stain is still there. And, my goodness, there's also this joy-soaked scene I never saw coming."

Because it's in the telling, in the opening, that we begin to see our stories for what they are—glory-filled and flawed works of art. We start giving (and, yes, getting) what all our tattered-cover lives really need.

Not comparison. A little more compassion.

Let's be the
HEROINES
in our own wild,
imperfect, *glorious* stories.
NEVER the understudies
for someone else's.

10

outside
the (Pink) Lines

> They weren't poised in flowery dresses giving professional talks about how to be better or stronger. Their lives were about how God had met them and was faithful in the broken places. Their stories, their lives, were their messages.
>
> —Sheila Walsh

I MISCARRIED JUST BEFORE EASTER. It seemed like a cruel paradox that all the world around me was bursting with new life and my body couldn't contain one. Just weeks before, I had stared in wonder at the double pink lines on a pregnancy test. I did an exuberant, awkward dance in front of the mirror and tried to come up with the perfect way to tell my husband.

I thought of a card I'd written for DaySpring, where I was working at the time. It had a sketch of a little frog sitting on its papa's shoulders and said, "I've got a lot of growing to do if my heart's gonna hold all my love for you." I found a pen and changed the ending to "Happy *Becoming a* Father's Day." I handed it to Mark on the back porch of our house on the first day the weather was warm enough to sit outside after a long winter. He'd just had knee surgery and couldn't get up to hug me, so he pulled me onto his lap with a relieved, delighted smile.

Those double pink lines had been almost two years in the making. And in only a few days they would be replaced by stunning, heartbreaking red.

Christmas morning that year I woke up early and slipped into the bathroom. I felt sure this would be the month, the redeeming and the new beginning. I'd already played it out in my mind. Everyone would open their presents and then I would say, "We have one more gift for all of you!" Mark and I would grin and tell them how God had answered our prayers, how everything would be all right now.

But before I even got the pregnancy test box open, that vision had been shattered. Mark came in to find me slumped against the bathroom wall, still in my wrinkled pajamas, face in my hands. I soaked his white T-shirt with tears while he held me. Every Christmas song I heard that day felt like a lie. Every present I opened seemed empty. I knew a baby had come for me long ago, but I wanted another one. And, just as much, I wanted to stop hoping.

Because hope is what breaks your heart, splits it wide open like the poor turkey on the table. And you are there, bare and exposed, for everyone to see your loss and disappointment and the cavern of almost abandoned dreams. The clichés don't cut it. The sermons don't cover it. It's just raw and unsightly, and you want to slip it into the trash and slam the lid forever. But at the end of the day, you fall asleep with a stack of tissues by your bed and wake up to hope again tomorrow. And if you do this long enough, it changes you—for better or worse.

I did it for almost a decade.

I'm saying this in case you are stretched out between desire and loss right now, stuck in the in-between of a dream. I could skip that last part and go straight to the better ending, to how it all turns out. But that middle place is the hardest—it's the furnace and the refinery and what remakes us. It's the labor and the sweat and the groaning. It can't be skipped or minimized, diminished or forgotten. It matters and is to be honored.

But it is also not the end.

So let me tell you the rest.

God, in all his mystery and knowing, in his tenderness toward what we really need, began gently showing me I didn't have to bear a physical child to still be a mother. Around Mother's Day the year after my miscarriage, he pointed me to Genesis, where Eve is called "the mother of all the living" (3:20). And I realized all women bring life to the world in some way.

I've birthed twelve books since then. A mama to a dozen. When *You're Already Amazing* released, my sweet small group threw me a book shower because they knew I'd never gotten to have a baby shower.

More Easters, Christmases, and Mother's Days came, went, were celebrated and mourned. Then one night I saw a documentary on television about foster kids who age out of the system. At eighteen they're simply told the equivalent of "have a nice life." I shook my head at the screen while saying over and over, "That's not okay." When people asked if we'd thought about adoption, I began to answer, "If we adopt, our kid will be a twenty-year-old." One day a friend of mine replied to that unusual response with, "Do you know about Saving Grace?" It turned out a transitional living home for girls who were aging out of the foster system or who would otherwise be homeless was being built right in my town.

I sent an out-of-the-blue email to Becky, Saving Grace's founder, that said something like, "I have this crazy dream of adopting a twenty-year-old . . ." Since she was right in the middle of a crazy dream herself, she let me come over. We sat on the lid of an ice chest in a living room still under construction and talked about our outlandish, almost impossible hopes.

Then life got busier for both of us, and I settled into raising my book babies. A few years later, in the fall just before my birthday, Becky reached out and asked if I'd like to come to a banquet celebrating the accomplishments of the girls in the program. God had impressed on my heart that my word for the next year was to be "love." And that evening at Saving Grace, I met a twenty-year-old named Lovelle. She wore a tilted tiara, a fancy dress, and an unforgettable smile. Looking back on that now makes me laugh because she's far more likely to be found in running gear or skinny jeans.

All the Saving Grace girls got a copy of my devotional *Opening the Door to Your God-Sized Dream*, and a few days later Lovelle texted me to say she liked it. We began a conversation and eventually I asked if she wanted to have lunch. I showed up at Saving Grace and discovered her at the kitchen table, craft supplies spread out everywhere, distracted and halfway through a project. At some point she asked if we had kids and I gave her the short version. When I left Saving Grace after lunch, she said simply, "Well, you can just be my mom."

Over the next few months, we began spending more time together and Mark met her as well. She couldn't understand why we wanted to be with her. Why we showed up at the finish line of her half marathon. Why we invited her into our home and our lives. Why we didn't seem to be going away.

But somewhere in the middle of a whole bunch of ordinary life, it became clear we were meant to be a family. She changed her last name legally to ours and eventually moved into a bedroom at our house. One night she came in late and accidentally dropped ice on the floor in the kitchen. Hearing the noise, I went to check on her and found her terrified, certain we would kick her out for that innocent offense.

That was the hardest part—her difficulty believing we really loved her, we wanted her, she was safe, and there would always be grace. Watching her wrestle with all of this gave me a taste of what God must feel with me sometimes.

Lovelle met my family in person for the first time at my grandpa Hollie's funeral (yep, I'm named after him). At the service each of the great-grandchildren was given a Bible belonging to my grandparents, and the minister offered a blessing, passing on their spiritual legacy. Lovelle sobbed on my shoulder and said, "God finally answered my prayers."

Around the same time Lovelle met us, she also met a boy. A little over a year later I watched her walk down the aisle as a giddy, glowing bride on the arm of my husband, her dad. The two of them danced to Selah's "Bless the Broken Road" at the reception, and right before it ended, I joined them. We stood in a circle, arms around each other, standing on the sacred ground of redemption.

It turns out Lovelle and I have similar passions, including writing and encouraging women. We even shared our story together several times last year at conferences for women. She interned for DaySpring, the same company where I started my career—where I wrote that card with the little frog on it.

And we're not the only ones with similarities in our new family. Lovelle married a thoughtful, steady auditor—the same personality type and occupation as my father. At holidays David and my father have a tendency to talk with excitement about enticing topics such as fraud cases and spreadsheets in a language only they fully understand.

There's more, so much more. Because, of course, God always knew.

For a long time I thought my happy ending needed to look the way this world told me it must and how I'd always imagined it. *Two pink lines.* But these days I'm discovering true joy in the messy, beautiful lines of a family love story I never expected.

Hope is not a liar.

11

Bone in the
chicken

> We risk being known as imperfect. We risk saying something we wish we hadn't. We risk showing others that we don't have it all together. But by taking these risks we discover that everybody else on the planet isn't perfect either. We discover that we can be ourselves—our imperfect, work-in-progress selves, and accept others in the process.
>
> —Suzie Eller

ONCE A MONTH, Mark and I bring dinner to Saving Grace, the transitional living facility for girls who age out of the foster system or would otherwise be homeless. The same one where we met our daughter, Lovelle. On Thursday nights, Saving Grace has "family dinner," where everyone gathers around the table. This may seem ordinary to most of us, but for many of the girls, it's the first time they've had this sort of experience.

I usually cook at home, then take the food to Saving Grace. The night before I did so for the first time, I made a quick stop at the grocery store to get last-minute ingredients. I'd just left a too-long event and was bleary-eyed and weary by the time I found myself in front of the meat section. I mindlessly grabbed a few packages of chicken thighs and headed out the door.

Now I am not a chef extraordinaire. When it comes to food, I've historically been far better at the eating than the making. In high school, my first attempts at cooking included adding tuna and a red sauce to boxed macaroni and cheese. It's as bad as you're imagining—possibly worse. When my husband and I married, I felt accomplished if I could open a bag from the freezer and get its contents to the table without burnt bits. I have made ciabatta bread so appalling even the dog wouldn't eat it. Yes, the same dog who gobbles up smelly things in the backyard on a regular and joyful basis.

But with patience, practice, and the Food Network, I have come a long way, baby. So by the time I signed up to bring dinner to Saving Grace, I thought not much in the culinary world could rattle me. Until I opened those packages of chicken thighs and stared at the contents in confusion and fear. I called my husband at work and he immediately sensed the panic in my voice. Most likely imagining a car wreck, terrible diagnosis, or burned-down house, he asked, "What's wrong?" I could barely speak the words. "There's a bone in the chicken." A quiet few seconds of confusion followed. Then a single word. "So?" Well, that just opened the floodgates. "I didn't know chicken thighs had a bone in them! The ones I've gotten before never did!" He pondered my sanity and the possibility that I'd been abusing a substance. Then, finally, in his ever-practical approach to life, he asked, "How do you think the chickens stand up?"

Looking back, I should have bust into gut-loud laughing in that moment. But I was too freaked out about serving up dinner to a group of new folks in a few hours, so I pressed on with all seriousness and inquired, "Well, what am I supposed to do?" He calmly explained I would need to cook the chicken thighs longer and that, no, the universe was not about to explode.

So I hung up the phone and began preparing the meal. It took forever and a day extra. I checked the chicken over and over—pink, pink, pink, right next to those sneaky bones. And I chose a maple-Dijon sauce that sloshed all over my kitchen, car, and pants. I smelled suspiciously like a cross between a pancake house and a hot dog stand. By the time I showed up at Saving Grace, stunned and breathless, everyone was already circled around the table. Seeing the look in my eyes, someone asked if I'd had an emergency. "Oh, no," I said. "It's just that there was a bone in the chicken." As if that explained everything. Bless their hearts for eating my food after I clearly announced I really didn't have a clue in the kitchen.

But you know what? In some ways, my answer does explain quite a bit. Because in this life, there is *surely* a bone in that chicken. Something we didn't expect. Something that interrupts our nice little timeline. Something that makes things messier and more frustrating and trickier than we thought they would be. Something that happens right when we want to impress everybody and humbles us instead. Something that makes us say, "Good grief, I am still so very human."

It turned out those silly bones didn't matter a bit. I set the dish on the table and everyone grabbed their portion. Bellies got fed, hearts got shared, and good things happened right there around what I thought to be proof that I should not be allowed to feed anyone ever again. Someone even asked for the recipe.

I'd considered, for a moment, not showing up. I figured they could order pizza and carry on without me. It would be fine. I could do it another time. But looking back, it wouldn't have been the same. In the eyes of those girls, me not showing up would have been one more adult not keeping their word. It would have been an opportunity missed because of my pride and desire to do it perfectly, to know everything. I wanted to play the role of Martha Stewart and all they really needed was plain ol' me.

Just this morning a dear friend and I talked about how choosing to be in community is not an easy thing. There are always surprises and a little chaos. We picture sharing life like a Thanksgiving spread from a magazine, but it can sometimes feel more akin to gathering around a TV tray with a microwave dinner gone slightly wrong. What matters is that we keep showing up. We keep releasing our vision of how we thought everything would go, how it would all unfold. We stop trying to be the heroines who save the day and instead just find our seats and say, "Yeah, me too." Then we find a way to talk about it. Or cry about it. Or giggle about it. Maybe all three at the same time, until our words stumble all over each other and our napkins have turned damp from our tears and our sides hurt from the laughing.

To this day, my daughter will still sometimes turn to me and say with a twinkle in her eyes, "Hey, Mom, there's a bone in the chicken." And we both smile at our secret joke, our wise little knowing. Oh yes, darling—turns out there always is.

shake the Jar

Even the smallest drop of God's strength is more than enough to cover our frailties, our shortcomings, the places where we deem ourselves weak.

—Lysa TerKeurst

I LEARNED TO MAKE BUTTER in Sunday school. Yep, that's how we roll in the South. It could have been a spiritual analogy or training up a child in the way she should go for potlucks. I'm entirely uncertain about the premise behind four-year-olds in a rainbow of plastic chairs shaking the daylights out of glass jars filled with cream. I only recall being awestruck when the contents changed, miraculously, into something entirely different. The preschool version of water into wine.

This is my first religious recollection (not surprising since I still tend to be motivated and impressed by free snacks). But I think perhaps there's another reason why my mind, which carelessly tosses out memories like old candy wrappers, kept this one.

Recently, my grown-up self seems perpetually impatient for my faith to be a solid, close-to-concrete thing. Butter bordering on brick. Something unchanging and reassuring in its constantness. I want edges and lines. Substance and form. I want to hold the final product in my hands.

Instead, it feels as if I'm forever shaking the jar. Questioning. Wondering. Wrestling. Struggling. Becoming. When I think I've gotten to a place where I have it figured out, I unscrew the lid only to realize what I thought could explain the entire universe and all of history is actually only able to cover half a biscuit. Every time that happens, I think, *I should be past this point by now*.

I grew up in church, after all. A sturdy, proper one with red brick and a white steeple and long wooden pews where I sat with my family each week. During the service, my younger brother and I took turns seeing which of us could find the most ancient song in the hymnal. Or I fidgeted with my mother's wedding ring, once sending it flying off her finger to land with a resounding "plunk" several rows in front of us. One Sunday what I heard from the pulpit officially became personal as I walked down the aisle to declare I had given my heart to Jesus.

Since then I've heard thousands more sermons, devoured stacks of books, gone to numerous conferences, and done enough Bible studies to qualify for some sort of Christian endurance medal. But still, on some days, like this one, I feel as if I know nothing. Not a thing. It's cream that slips right through my fingers, and I can't hold any of it at all.

I've been reading through the Old Testament for the first time in many years. The God I find there, especially in places like Leviticus and Numbers, sometimes seems utterly unknown to me. And the stories I've heard my whole life, first told on flannel boards by the kindest of women with the gentlest of voices, seem entirely different than the real, uncensored version right there on the pages. Then

I get scared that I've gotten it wrong, and yes, I must be perfect always because this God is so holy and I am unlike him in every way.

But the more I read the more I also discover this: God is absolutely committed to his plans. He is completely devoted to his promises. He is forever and ever faithful to what he's said he will do. This means, among other things, that *grace through faith* is as absolute as the law that came before it.

To be honest, it doesn't feel that way to me some days. So I've been known to live as if grace is for salvation but not for ordinary life. Not for the salty tears or the skinned knees or what makes us shout in the empty car. To help with all that, I make up lists of rules for myself, ways I think I can win God's approval. Being a church lifer means I've got more material stockpiled than a seminary. Everything has a potential "should." While this is a recipe for going full-out crazy, it's also oddly reassuring. I can be dry-eyed and put together and silent. Because I am creating my own kind of certainty.

But the process of faith, I'm finding, is not like my careful system. Instead, it's learning to live in the mystery. "Faith is confidence in what we hope for and assurance about what we do not see" (Heb. 11:1). Although it sounds similar, faith is an entirely different thing than logical, cold certainty. Instead, it's about a deep and wild security. After all, what I really hope for is not managing to finally follow my rules; it's to believe I'm truly loved anyway. What I want assurance about is not that I'm capable of being perfect but that someone will catch me when I fall. Every single time.

Maybe the little girl who twirls in her grape-juice-splattered skirt and holler-sings "Jesus loves me, this I know, for the Bible tells me so" is really so much wiser than I am with all my respectable lessons and learning. Maybe this is another example of what Jesus meant when he told us to have childlike faith. Not faith that completely understands but faith that trusts.

I've always been fond of a fluffy, lovely bow tied on a package. And that part of me would like very much to reassure you (and me) that I will get this whole faith thing wrapped up in the next few sentences or at least the next few decades. I will totally comprehend grace. I will have all my questions answered. I will no longer wrestle or struggle. But I'm coming to accept that's not how it is to be human. Things don't go that way in a world where everything good and beautiful is also humbling and inexplicable. None of us has everything figured out. Until heaven, we're all in this "not fully knowing" together, somewhere in the middle of the cream and butter. And this might be the surest thing I can say about living as people of faith: we hold on and shake the jar.

Flops and
rafters

This is the fiercest love I know. That while we were sinners, Christ died for us.

—Alia Joy Hagenbach

I HAD A COLOSSAL FAILURE THIS WEEK. A belly flop on the surface of life. The kind that makes the lifeguard in red shorts jump to attention. The sort that compels mamas to turn the pigtailed heads of their sweet children away so they won't witness the aftermath. The type that causes the kids who blow things up in backyards after school to stop and say, "Whoa," with an impressed and slightly envious look in their eyes.

I could not believe this happened. It was in an area of my life where I ride the same struggle like a merry-go-round. And I was sure, so sure that this time *I would not mess up again.* But of course I did.

Sitting in church the weekend after this failure, I looked up at the rafters and thought about how if I had to reach one to be good enough for God, then all my efforts so far have gotten me perhaps a few sorry centimeters high. I still jump and jump. I try and try. Sometimes I even feel proud because I seem to be getting just a bit more air than, oh, the ice-cream truck robbers and puppy snatchers. Other times I know folks are thinking the same about me. But in the end, none of us are really any closer.

In the middle of those thoughts, I unexpectedly thanked God for the first time ever for my area of struggle, the one I'd failed in this week. I don't believe he caused it, but I believe he has allowed it instead of annihilating it without any effort on my part. Because it has taken me right to the end of my own righteousness. It has been the thing I cannot beat. It has eaten my lunch and smacked me on the bottom and run over my noble intentions with a semitruck. And this has stunned me into seeing what I just couldn't or wouldn't before.

My husband and I have been watching a popular television show about a group of women. Being the queen of hypothetical questions, I asked him, "Which character am I most like?" I expected him to pick the one who always seems to be right in the middle of a mess. Instead, he said, "You're like so-and-so, who just wants to be perfect." Well, blow me over with a feather.

The next time I watched the show, I knew he was right. She was the one who tried to keep it all together. The one who voluntarily baked the twelve dozen cookies and double-checked her makeup in the car just before she went into the party and sometimes cried into her pillow at night because she hadn't yet told anyone the full extent of the latest drama in her life. Sometimes when I watch her, I want to say, "Bless your heart, stop trying so hard. You're going to make yourself crazy." I know this is good advice, because I say it often to myself.

But I'm learning not to play that role anymore. And after the service ended, as I was walking through the kiddie section, which smells like popcorn and floor cleaner, this odd prayer I had never said before popped into my mind. I suddenly asked, "Jesus, will you be good for me?" I didn't mean "good for me" in the way we say it about broccoli or wearing sunscreen. I meant it like, "Will you be good in my place? In other words, will you touch the rafters for me? Will you be perfect on my behalf? Will you cover over all the errors in the script of my life with the red pen that is the cross?"

And you know what? He said *yes*. Because the scandalous miracle of the gospel is that he *always* says yes to prayers like that one, however strangely worded or timed they may be.

I recently had a discussion with someone about what my tattoo would say if I ever got inked. I couldn't answer in any kind of satisfactory way (and it's unlikely I'd ever get one because I feel about needles the way others do about ten-foot snakes or plate-sized spiders). But after that prayer, I thought if I did get a tattoo, it would say, "By grace alone." Because it's the truth I most need to remember and most often forget. I have been a grace-plus girl. Grace plus my efforts. Grace plus my goodness. Grace plus my trying. All those pluses only subtract from what Jesus is freely giving me. What has already been mine for so very long.

After a few decades on this spinning earth, I am still so much of a mystery to myself. I stand at the end of the diving board, toes curled over the edge, and can't predict with any kind of accuracy how the next jump will go. I am the belly flopper and star performer, mess and perfectionist, struggler and self-sufficient desperado. I am paradox and contradiction, contrast and inconsistency. So much time, so many tries, and this is all I'm sure is true of all of me: every part of who I am needs Jesus more than I even fully understand, more than I can really find the right words to say.

Let's be *gentle* with *each other* and *ourselves*,
tender toward our failures.
It can be an *act of worship*
to remember we are **only human**,
not **GOD** after all.

Praying
wronger

Being brave doesn't mean you aren't scared, it just means you keep fighting for hope and praying for miracles.

—Robin Dance

I DON'T ALWAYS KNOW how to pray properly. Or at least that's how it feels on occasion. Some folks might point me to the Lord's Prayer and say, "Well, there's your answer." And I understand they would do so with the best of intentions. But when the disciples said, "Teach us to pray," and Jesus gave that prayer as the response, I don't think he meant for it to be a one-size-fits-all-forever formula. I think he meant it as a model, one we continue to figure out how to apply to our flesh-and-sweat lives. This is the part where I can get confused.

The first time I remember praying a real, official prayer was in the bedroom of my grandparents' home where I stayed when my family visited. Originally a closet, it had just enough space for a little wooden bed and a spot on the floor to play with my mother's childhood toys. The room was the perfect size for a granddaughter, like having a sleepover in a dollhouse. The bed had a square shelf built right into the headboard, and my grandparents kept a tiny Bible there. I remember opening that Bible one day and reading a few lines. I told God then and there I wanted Jesus to be my Savior and for him to have my whole heart, for my whole life. The next Sunday, I sprinted down the red-carpeted church aisle to share this decision with friends and family.

Fast-forward a few years to an evening when I was on my bike, a solo explorer of the golf course around the corner. The golfers had likely retreated to dinners or beers at the club, so I had the entire wondrous and usually forbidden place to myself. The sun was just starting to finger paint the clouds orange and yellow and red. I felt God so near, so very close, as though he were sitting on the handlebars of my pink bike.

Come to think of it, I don't think I said much at all during that bike ride. It's actually a bit strange that I still consider it one of the primary examples of prayer in my life. But that's the thing—I'm not a talker by nature. The folks I tend to feel most comfortable with are those who can let stretches of silence into our times together. The ones who don't ask, "What's wrong?" or try to force me to converse when I have not a thing to say.

But prayer, I have been taught at times, is about a whole lot of talking. Some folks are comfortable being verbally sparring prayer warriors with lists like weapons. I've been instructed to pray using acronyms that take me through a series of requests and proclamations. In groups, it can sometimes seem like the person who prays the loudest or longest is setting the example to follow.

I'm not saying prayer tools and techniques can't be helpful. It's just that if I'm not careful, they can also contribute to my prayers feeling far less than perfect. My prayers naturally lean more toward how I connect with people in real life. The words matter, but they aren't the *only* thing. Often what's truly really important is just being in each other's presence.

Lately I've been trying to force myself to pray the way I think I'm supposed to. But I keep going back to simple things, like "Thank you" and "Please" and "I love you." At night I lie in bed and think about the day. I ponder and process. It feels like God and I are having coffee the way I do with good friends. But it's messy and ordinary and seems to be missing a lot of the spiritual words I've learned I'm supposed to use when I pray. It feels like it doesn't quite count.

But maybe it does. Maybe what I really want is not to be able to pray better but for my life to become a prayer. *My whole life*. When I'm standing in the grocery store line or typing on a keyboard or answering the phone to hear the most difficult news.

I love my husband very much, but if someone gave me all kinds of rules for how I had to talk to him, it would stress me out and shut me up. I would become focused on my performance instead of our connection. I would miss the times just sitting on the porch staring at the trees, listening to his breath as we fall asleep, or laughing at nothing important on the TV.

I think maybe there are all kinds of communication and all kinds of prayers. And God knows his children because he made us, so he's okay with us praying *as we are* rather than the way someone else tells us we must. I have dear friends who love structure in their prayer time. They're also the shelf organizers and bullet-point users who keep the world turning on its axis. I have friends who enjoy praying aloud and have plenty to say. They're my beloved extroverts who fill the void with their vibrant words wherever they go. This makes a lot of good sense to me.

I got to be at my grandpa Hollie's side when he stepped across the threshold to Home, to where praying is also seeing. In some ways, the experience felt so familiar. A little bed. A quiet room. A Bible close by. Except instead of me giving my heart to Jesus, this time my grandpa was entering the forever reality of that long-ago decision in his own life. I held his hand and flipped through photos of us together on my phone. I listened to worship music as the sun set on my grandpa's earth time (a sunrise somewhere else). And suddenly I felt an entirely unexpected, completely inexplicable peace and joy. It was as if God lifted the hem of heaven for a moment and let me experience just a glimpse, just a taste of what my grandpa would soon fully embrace. It felt like sacred ground, like a thin place.

I don't remember the actual words I spoke to God then—if I said any at all—but in all the ways that matter most, I think of those moments as a prayer marker in my grown-up life. And perhaps, in the end, sharing all of life with God is what praying really means. It's that line, "Thy Kingdom come, Thy will be done."[1] It's not about getting what we want or proving something to God. Instead, it's about aligning our hearts with his. It's about *heaven-come-here*.

I think sometimes prayer is beautiful and sometimes it's downright hard. Sometimes it's full of happiness and sometimes it's overflowing with tears. Sometimes it's about order and ritual and sometimes it's about being a wreck on our knees in front of the God who loves us anyway.

I don't think I will ever totally pray correctly. Because I'm coming to believe there isn't any such thing. I've heard the best marriages are like a lifelong conversation with stops and starts, pauses and surprises, tears and laughter, sorrow and great gladness. I think maybe this is how prayer is too. It's really just a lifelong conversation with someone we love.

When we forget that, when we make prayer a task to be done in a certain way, we can miss the point entirely. And all the while, God is standing right there in front of us, holding out his hand to us because he just wants to walk us Home.

Let us pray.

room for Knobs

God gave us each one unique life. Meant to be lived out in our actual situations. I don't want the gifts he's offered to go unnoticed nor the opportunities wasted. I want to live into where he's called me and me alone.

—Alexandra Kuykendall

I STAND OVER A STOVE and the sizzle of maple bacon in a pan. I watch as the color goes from pink to amber to crusty brown. I make room for eggs, winding their sunny yellow centers into deep green spinach. I plate it all with a companionable piece of wheat toast, butter spread like frosting over the top. And then, as a last-minute addition, I scoop up a small bowl of fruit—blushing red strawberries and moody blackberries. Oh yes, let's also have that coffee that smells as though a slice of vanilla cake has vanished right into the cup.

I try to balance all this abundance and head toward the patio. But when I come to the slightly ajar door, I realize my hands are too full to turn the knob. I stand there for what feels like a lengthy amount of time and nudge a corner with my foot, hoping it will open. But no luck. So I reluctantly set my coffee on a nearby table and in two and a half seconds I'm outside.

As I take my seat, coffee retrieved, I laugh a bit at myself. Because this is how I go through life so often. I think I have to hold on to it all, all the time. I act like setting something down means it's lost to me forever—gone down some dark cosmic hole—when most likely it's just sitting on the edge of the table right where I left it. I can go back for it when I'm ready, when it's time.

I'm on the wooden deck of my friend's lake house this morning as I think about all this. The water is spread out in layers of blue and the birds are saying their hellos and stop that's and I love you's from branches all around me. There's also a lawn mower next door I'm trying hard to ignore while simultaneously wondering if silencing it with a sledgehammer would mean I'd go to jail. Ah, it must have sensed the threat—all quiet again now.

It's the third year my friend and I have come here to write for a few days. Our routine is usually the same—the bacon in the pan and the typing on the patio and fruity sorbet in front of nineties television reruns in the evening after our minds have worn themselves out like children at an all-day birthday party.

When you come back to the same place this way, it becomes a sort of marker in your life. Because while the everyday blurs together, I can sit here and clearly remember, *Last time I was at the lake house, this or that was going on.* The previous two years I sat on that deck and pondered some kind of perceived-to-be-crisis/opportunity situation in my life. Something that had my insides pounding like waves against a dock when an unruly boat zips by. Now, with the benefit of distance, I can see both of those scenarios were not worth the emotion or energy I gave them. In reality, what I needed to do was set them down like my coffee cup and let them be. I needed to take my given plate and walk through the door to what was next, trusting I would not miss out if I did so.

I recently had a conversation with someone about the current "fomo" trend in our culture. On the off chance you're a bit slang illiterate (like me), fomo stands for "fear of missing out." That phrase shows up right now on social media and at trendy get-togethers (which might be why I didn't know the meaning) and in the midnight hour when we stare at the ceiling. I've heard it said in different ways from stay-at-home mamas, corporate climbers, pink-mohawked hipsters, and silver-haired retirees. It is a fear we all have in common. It has been part of my own inner vocabulary too. And it has contributed to me jostling dinnerware and hot mugs like a bad waiter while trying to open doors with my left pinky toe.

In that conversation about the infamous and universal fomo, I said, "I have worried about what I might miss out on if I don't hold on to everything. But I have never thought about the other risk—the one that's actually much more likely to happen—and that's if I live that way, I will certainly miss out on at least some of what's right in front of me."

If I stand inside the door because I can't set anything down, even for a moment, I will miss out on the lake in the morning light, the squirrel that recklessly runs the railing right in front of me like a teenage show-off, the words to be created and exchanged later with my friend like braided neon bracelets in junior high.

Believing we can have it all, all the time is a myth and a lie and a joy stealer. What I do believe is that we can have God's best for us. *A full life and life to the full are two very different things.* One is about grasping, the other is about receiving. One is about cram-ming in, the other is about room to breathe. One is about striving, the other is about trust. One is about control, the other is about letting go—sometimes for a moment and sometimes for always.

I am slowly learning to be a woman who has the gumption (as we say in the South) to set things down so she may move forward, so she may be present. This, I am surprised to find, is much scarier than trying to balance it all. I feel safer with my hands latched on to as much as they can possibly hold. But when I live that way, there is no turning of knobs, not much space left for the hand of God in mine.

On my bravest and truest days, this is my tiny manifesto for the begging calendar and needy to-do list and noisy-noisy internet: I do not want to come to the end of life and say, "I didn't miss out on anything." What I'm aiming to say is, "I missed out on exactly the right things."

wearing the Hat

> No brave person has not known fear.
> It's what we do with our fear that determines our course.
>
> —Meredith Bernard

ON THE VERY TOP SHELF OF MY CLOSET sits a white woven basket full of hats. A gray wool one with thin, blue stripes. A fluffy crocheted one with a single red flower. A brown plaid with a button on the brim. Next to this basket, all on its own, sits a single hat. It has gathered dust for more than a decade. I've thought of giving it away a hundred times. But I've not been able to bring myself to do it.

This hat is not as lovely as its assortment of sisters. More functional than stylish. A plain black ball cap with a single word stitched neatly across the front in white letters. And it is this word that has kept me from the wearing. It says simply and without apology, "writer." All the attendees at a writers' conference where I taught a workshop years ago received one. The instant I saw it I loved it. But for so long I would not, could not bring myself to put it on and step into public.

Until yesterday.

Last summer, to my great surprise, I started running. But then cold weather arrived and I decided I would stick to the warm, cozy back room of my house and the soft-cushioned stationary bike in it. Yesterday marked the official kickoff of a new summer, and I made a goal of beginning to run again. But the skies did not cooperate with my plan and insisted on a slow, lazy drizzle. Finally enough was enough and I went searching in my closet for attire that would let me go anyway. I needed some layers and, to keep the rain out of my eyes, a hat.

Of all the hats available to choose from, only one would do. I picked up the "writer" hat, plopped it on my head, pulled my ponytail through the little opening in the back, and headed out the door.

And I ran.

As I did, I thought about how this kind of scenario is true for so many of us. It's the cliché, we all have so many hats we wear— mom, daughter, friend, employee, wife, sister. These are beautiful and noble and keep the world spinning. And everything I'm going to say next mostly applies to them too. But I want to talk especially about the other hat, the one still on the shelf all by itself. We look at it sometimes and wonder what it would be like to wear it. But we don't touch it. We leave it be. Because our hat says a scary word. A word like "writer" or "fighter" or "leader" or "dreamer" or "mentor" or "encourager" or "wedding-cake maker" or "_____" (put yours here). The thing we both secretly long for and are terrified by.

If you've got a hat like this, then you know it already. And if there's not such a hat in your collection, that's okay too. This is still for you because someone you love has one, and they're going to need you to understand.

When we look at the hat, we imagine what people will think when they see us in it. I always did with mine. I pictured putting it on my head, walking out the door, and taking a seat at a little café to work. I thought of folks at other tables pointing and whispering, "She's probably not a *real* writer." Or asking with a bit of scorn, "Who does she think she is?"

But here's the thing: someone gave me the hat. Someone said, "You are worthy to wear this." And someone might have put a hat like that on the shelf of your closet too. The Creator of all things has bestowed it on you. The gift itself is the only requirement for you to use it. *Who do I think I am? Who do you think you are?* We are the image bearers of a star-scattering, water-walking, miracle-making God. We have every right to wield with force and holy wildness all he has placed within us.

If we manage to pick up that hat, to hold it in our hands for a moment, to consider it, then we will look out the window and it will be raining. So we will check the forecast over and over again as we tell ourselves that *later* will be better. Not now. Not in the middle of all this. And there is a time for being still, for waiting. But if we know that this is not what we are doing, that we are simply delaying because we're scared or feeling a bit inadequate, then it's time to go anyway.

Because wearing that hat is not about perfect conditions. It's about showing up in spite of them. This is what I have learned: yes, talent and education and preparation can be helpful tools, but they are not as helpful as flat-out grit. They will not get us as far as putting one foot in front of the other and simply refusing to quit. None of us are ready. All of us are afraid. This does not change no matter how long we have been at it or how much success we've experienced. Living on the edge of our knowing and beating down the fear over and over are part of progress-making. Our role is simply not to let them control or defeat us, not to trip us up or keep us paralyzed with our hand forever on the front door knob.

I also did not want to put on that hat because I kept thinking of all the folks who could wear it so much better. I almost dropped it in the mail to friends several times. Friends whose words are like art in the museum case or hot bread fresh from the oven or a mama lullaby for the soul. I thought *they* should have it. I'd forgotten I serve the abundant God who sprinkles golden sand across a thousand shores, who watches over the sparrows hatching on a million spring green limbs, who sketches fiery sunrises onto the horizon every day and everywhere. He is the hat giver. And he has one or a dozen for all of us. They are not better or worse than anyone else's. They are simply ours.

So we bravely decide to put on the hat and make it to the sidewalk and start to move. At this moment it is almost certain we will hear "stop!" in a hundred ways. The neighbor's Chihuahua will bark and suddenly look to us like a Doberman. Our big toe will get a new ache and we will be sure it's a terminal disease. The hill will have grown steeper overnight. The terrible little children who live in the house on the corner will make faces out the window. We will be tempted to take all this as a sure sign that we have, indeed, been presumptuous and foolish. Surely it is better to turn around now before it gets worse. We will try again another time.

But this assault is part of the process. No matter if we wait a day, a week, or half a century, it will still come. Because when we do what is life-giving and worthwhile and beautiful, we will always face resistance. This is affirmation that we are on our way.

And these inconveniences, annoyances, and obstacles will not stop if we keep going. They may even get worse. This is not to discourage you; it is to inform you. Because if we do not expect them, if we do not know they are universal and inevitable, then we will take them personally. But all this is not about us. It is part of a war story that has been unfolding since the beginning of time. And the hat that looks so innocent is actually the warrior's helmet. We are making a declaration when we wear it. And everything that is in opposition to what is good takes notice of such things.

I finished running my route eventually. Soaked. Mud-spattered. Smelling terrible. None of it mattered. I'd made it home. "I have fought the good fight, I have finished the course, I have kept the faith" (2 Tim. 4:7 NASB). At the end of my days, I want not perfection but completion, not to be flawless but to have remained faithful, not to show up squeaky clean but to come to heaven's doorstep sweaty and spent, having dared to put on that hat too—the one I almost didn't wear at all.

17

shiny rocks

Sometimes I like to dream about what the world would be like if we all chose to believe that how God made us is entirely good enough. . . . You have so much to offer the world: beauty and art and rare gifts that can only come from your hands, your voice, your beautiful brain. But ultimately you have to choose to believe that.

—Aliza Latta

SHE ASKS THE USUAL QUESTIONS, rushed and fervent. "How do I get published? How can I build my platform? What made you successful?" I can see the desperation and disappointment darting from behind her words. The insecurity and fear and jealousy she's trying to stuff back in like feral kittens in a box. *She doesn't really mean to act like this,* I try to tell myself. *This reaction isn't really about me.* But a lie comes hissing toward my ear, its tiny claws against my neck, saying, "The good in your life makes people feel bad."

I know this is trickery and mockery. I can trace its winding path all the way back to junior high when a friend, a dear one, announced one day the cause of her daggered eyes and snide remarks: jealousy. I felt small and ashamed and chastised then. The same way I do now with this girl who wants to talk about words and how hers might stand as tall as skyscrapers, as high as a monument, so everyone can see them.

In the past, I have let that lie bow my head and put its fingers over my lips. "Don't tell them the happy news," it whispers into my ear. "Don't share what went well." If I carried on, the voice would get louder, "Selfish. Prideful. Inconsiderate."

But now, on the periphery of middle age, I am tired of all this. I am sick of it like the last bite of a pizza sticking to the box. It tastes old and stale and unfortunate in my mouth. It belongs only in the trash can with the banana peels and yesterday's newspaper and paper towels covered in spaghetti sauce.

Because here is the truth: What's in my life is not about me. It's about the Maker and the Bestower and the Shaper of all.

I went to summer camp only one time. The camp was in West Texas, a place where the rocks jutted and the creeks ran clear. Where we had nightly meetings in a revival-style building without walls so that the crickets joined the choir. I'd never been to such a place and felt taken with everything, from the scratched wooden bunk beds to the instant mashed potatoes. I looked up at the stars, feeling swollen with wonder, and it seemed God tenderly whispered to my heart, "Always remember to love the Giver more than the gifts."

It struck me, this statement, because in my young mind, it was the first time I'd drawn a straight line from every blessing I had to the One who had offered them. It made sense to me, this way of thinking, and that moment would come back to me again and again through the years.

I have forgotten this moment at times too. I have grasped and snatched, coveted and stolen, compared and warred for what I wanted. I have been Gollum from Lord of the Rings, eyes glittering with madness. "My precious," I have said. In other words, I have made an idol of what is only a trinket. Only a symbol or keepsake.

It would make no sense to become more enamored with my wedding ring than with my husband. But I have done this with what God has placed in my hands. I think it is this knowing, this having been there myself, that makes me cringe when someone asks those questions about publishing and confesses her longing for what I have. "More," we say. "Tell me how to get more."

But we don't realize it will never be enough. If we could point a divine vacuum at the target of our envy and pull from her everything we think would make us whole, we would only and always find we are still hollow. Because that kind of desire is a bottomless pit, a greedy wasteland, a black hole swirling in our universe.

The woman I'm meeting with is looking at me now, pen poised over paper. She wants to take notes and make plans. She is waiting, waiting for me to let the secret slip. She's watching for the magic potion to be pulled from my pocket. "Drink this," I will say, "and your words will be immortal." But I don't have any magic potion to offer. So I say the only thing I know to be true: "Our role is obedience; God's job is results. It's all about loving him and the people he entrusts to us. Serve whoever is right in front of you, and he will make a way."

She is disappointed and lowers her pen. I watch her consider what I've said, that there might be a different approach than the one she lugged in with her, so heavy. She's wrestling right in front of me, loosening the fingers wrapped around its handle, but she's not ready to set it down. Not today. Instead, she asks, "But wasn't there something that gave you your big break?"

I think later of how what we so often need is not a big break but to be broken. To come to the place where we are disappointed by all we've been chasing, when we're humbled and exhausted, hungry and fed up with ourselves. When we finally throw what we have grasped in our hands against the wall so that it shatters to pieces. Because only then are our hands empty again. Empty to be truly filled.

This is what I wish for her, this woman sitting across from me, that God will do in her life what he did in mine—rescue her from herself and her desires. That he will speak to her under starry night skies and guard her when the spotlight is so bright it threatens to sunburn her soul. That he will woo her and chase her and never give up on her, never stop convincing her of who she really is and what she really wants.

We can imagine ourselves to be the proud explorers planting the flags on the tops of mountains. Sultans piling our treasures high. Safe-crackers chiseling our way into the secrets that will make us happy. But we sometimes miss that we can also be the toddlers not yet knowing the mountain is an anthill, the treasure plastic, and the safe a Cracker Jack box.

As we understand the situation better, we can be tempted to think God must want less for us than we want for ourselves. Otherwise the prayers would be answered, the wishes granted, the gold more than shiny rocks. But the opposite is true. It's not that the God who loves us doesn't want us to dream big; it's that he understands better than any of us that any gift but all of *him* is small.

He would not have us settle.

18

Red
teapot

I REMOVE THE BUBBLE WRAP SLOWLY, pushing against the cylinders with childlike fingers, remembering the sensation and *pop* that delighted me years ago. At this moment I'm too eager to be distracted, so I snip through the tape and then slide it all aside without hesitation. I lift the cardboard lid and reach inside. When I catch the first glimpse of it, I gasp. It's *red*, like date-night lipstick or a toy fire truck or the most audacious of summer flowers. From the outside image, I'd assumed it was white. Lovely and endearing in its simplicity. But I am delighted that it's turned out to be my favorite color instead.

I hold the teapot like I would a small, tame animal and stroke it. My husband shakes his head, mystified by this display. But he has long since stopped trying to understand. He's just happy that I'm happy. And clearly this teapot has done the trick.

I have only recently discovered tea. For most of my life it has been coffee, coffee, coffee. I thought tea came only in boring little paper packets and tasted always like slightly modified water. But then I discovered loose leaf tea—an array of flavors and smells and moods. Just yesterday I had an apple caramel almond tea scented like nuts roasted in the open air at the yearly autumn fair held in a nearby field. I hung my head over the rim of my mug and breathed memories, soft like scarves, crisp like wind.

It's been a revelation, this tea. And, yes, I realize gushing about loose leaf tea may not make the cool list, but I have come to the point in my life where I have decided to love what I love and not be ashamed of it. I think, perhaps a bit naively, there is something endearing and backboned in this.

I discover my little teapot has a loose leaf tea infuser right there in the middle of it. You simply place the tea inside the infuser and then pour hot water over it. Whatever flavor is on the inside comes out—citrus or cinnamon, earthy green or smooth chamomile, delicate white pomegranate or bold peppermint.

We, as humans, are not unlike this. "What you say flows from what is in your heart" (Luke 6:45). This has implications I'm pondering these days. Because it seems the twin myths we believe are these: *I control how other people respond. Other people control how I respond.* I've become convinced these assumptions are responsible for so much of the heartbreak and chaos and shattered windows in this world.

A woman walks through the door of my counseling office, her shoulders stooped and face lined with worry. I watch her eyes dart around the room as if someone might jump out from a corner any moment. I ask her about her concerns and she says, "I'm not a good enough wife. No matter how hard I try I can't make my husband happy. I put dinner on the table and it's too hot or too cold. I slip on lingerie and I'm too curvy in some places and too flat in others. I say the wrong things at the wrong time. I need to get better." This woman doesn't realize yet that in the center of her husband's teapot, in the depths of his heart, is something bitter and dark called "unpleasable."

A different woman announces her arrival at my office with the staccato stomp of her boots against the floor. She throws open the door and huffs at me, though I've not yet said a word. I ask what she'd like to work on and she waves away the question. "Oh," she says, "I'm not here for me." Then she tells me about a husband who sits on the couch and a daughter who slams the bathroom door and drivers like ancient tortoises on the interstate. She has issues with her preacher and her plumber and her second cousin with the big ears and dyed red hair she hasn't seen for twenty years. "If they would all just get their acts together, then I wouldn't be this way," she concludes. She doesn't understand how the acridness of her attitude taints her relationships.

These examples are extreme, but we're all affected by what we allow into our hearts and minds. In *Invisible Influence*, researcher Jonah Berger asserts that far more of what we think and feel is predetermined than we realize. We consider every thought and action to be instant and independent. We are not easily swayed, we would say. Yet he tells how two groups of people were told to review a list of words. The first group was given a list of negative words, such as *reckless* and *aloof*. The second group had positive words, such as *daring* and *brave*.

Both groups then read a story about a man who had climbed Mount McKinley, driven in a demolition derby, and was now considering crossing the Atlantic in a sailboat. When asked to describe the man, those who had read the first list did so negatively while the second group saw him in a positive light—the rugged adventurer. Everyone involved in the experiment considered themselves unbiased and objective. But the "tea" already inside their minds, for better or worse, tainted the outcome.

I've lived a version of this experiment. On any particular day I can write what seems to me to be a perfectly benign blog post. Neither the greatest nor worst I've ever done. And it's quite possible I will get two entirely different responses. One will inform me my approach is too grace-based. And the other will ask if I can please ease up a bit.

I love my readers and want to serve well with my words, so this feedback usually makes me scratch my head and stare at my keyboard. If the words are harsh, I might also consider moving to Australia and becoming a barista. But this solution is not hazard-proof either. I picture the line, the person in front who thinks the cappuccino has too much foam and the one behind them whining because it has too little. The customer who says the cake from the glass case has gobs of icing and the other who hollers because we're skimping. After about a dozen imaginary people, I shrug my shoulders in surrender and go back to typing.

In other words, there's no escape hatch from being an opinionated human surrounded by opinionated humans. I think this is an important thing to know because it lets us shift the myths we talked about before to what actually makes sense, what God tells us. These are the twin truths that can help us love and serve folks so much better: *I do not control how other people respond. Other people do not control how I respond.*

Regarding the first statement, we get confused sometimes and think loving means making everyone happy. But we have no power of this kind. We might as well say loving means making the sun rise. What loving does mean is being intentional in the way we treat those around us. We alone control what's inside of us. And what's inside is always what comes out.

To say it straight, every day we're pouring water into other people's teapots and they into ours. We can drive ourselves half mad trying to alter this reality, but doing so is optional. Accepting this is both a relief and a responsibility.

Once on a blue-sky fall afternoon, a friend of mine and I wandered into a local tea shop. The walls were lined with small sample packets of loose leaf. We oohed and aahed over flavors like chocolate and peach and ginger-lemon. We talked about which one would be nice for breakfast and what we'd pair with a blueberry scone and which we'd sip before bedtime while we read a book. Then we chose for ourselves.

And this is the miracle of our hearts too: *we get to choose*. We can have kindness and patience and the sweetness of peace. We can have the hardiness of courage and faith like wildflowers. Or we can have the sharpness of fear and the sourness of jealousy. Pride like a wet, dirty sock and disdain like old paint thinner. Perhaps the reality is we are all a blend of so many things. "Taste and see that the LORD is good" (Ps. 34:8) sounds like a fitting declaration, a worthy invitation for all of us.

I tip my little red pot and the tea spills out into my cup. I take a sip and it's as I anticipated—warm and strong and true. It feels like hope stirred with a spoon, like a prayer about who I want to be.

P.S. For no other reason than to make you smile: One Friday evening I asked my husband to take me to an outdoor shopping area to stock my tea stash. After we left an adorable little store with a bag full of goodness, I asked if he'd like to walk around for a while.

I jokingly said, "Come on, let's live on the edge a little."

"Well, we already bought loose leaf tea, didn't we?" he responded.

I considered the implications of this question. "So if our tea is living loose, then so are we?"

He nodded. I laughed.

I love that man.

Like Water
into wine

I think we . . . have failed to notice the same Lord
God who gave us the strength to work and the
wrinkles to frown also gave us the legs to dance
and the voices to sing!

—Inge Marie's grandma in the children's book
When Mischief Came to Town

ON MY WEDDING DAY I said an enthusiastic "Oh yeah!" instead of a calm and proper "I do." I startled the preacher as well as the crowd, who sat in stunned silence for a second before breaking out into nervous giggles. It felt as if everyone thought I might be in a bit of trouble. But the traditional, formal words just weren't quite enough right then. I needed something a bit more expressive, a little more from the gut and the heart. So this quiet introvert hollered at the altar in her white lace dress. And I've never regretted it.

I was reminded of this recently at the wedding of the niece of dear friends who are like family to me and Mark. The ceremony was short and sweet. The reception was long and loud. Along with our friends, we found a spot on the edge of the dance floor. We watched as the wedding party alternately swayed and stomped, line danced, and raised their hands in the air as they shouted the lyrics to favorite songs. Ties got loosened, shoes came off, and sweat glistened on smiling faces. Glasses were raised and the cake was cut. We didn't get home until almost one o'clock in the morning.

As I lay in bed that night I thought about how Jesus chose to begin his public ministry at a marriage celebration. Jewish weddings at that time were exuberant events full of feasting and celebrating. There would have been music and dancing, laughter and embracing, delicious food and vats of wine.

It's not what I would expect. When I imagine Jesus coming into this scene it's easier to picture him standing with crossed arms as he surveys the room. I think of him whispering to the disciples something about "inappropriate behavior." I picture them nodding in agreement before he steps up to the soundboard to press the off button so a proper prayer meeting can commence. Or at the very least I would guess if someone walked up to Jesus and said, "They're out of wine," his response would be to pull out the coffee or tea or whatever the ancient equivalent might be. Then send everyone home to do some holy homework. Something more spiritual. Serious. Substantial. Instead, in a move that still has me scratching my head, he makes *more* wine so the party can keep going.

When I look at the Old Testament, I see more of the same. Take this example in which God instructed the Israelites about what to do with their tithes: "Use the silver to buy whatever you like: cattle, sheep, wine or other fermented drink, or anything you wish. Then you and your household shall eat there in the presence of the LORD your God and rejoice" (Deut. 14:26).

I have quietly and perhaps scandalously pondered something with people in one-on-one conversations for years. It concerns me deeply, but I've never been brave enough to ask it publicly. I'm going to now: *Have we, perhaps, forgotten how to party in God's name?*

I don't mean the stereotypical "partying," not the Mardi Gras mayhem or teenagers taking advantage of parents being gone for a weekend. I mean knowing how to surrender to joy and all the good gifts God offers. I believe a part of us is made for sanctified wildness. There's something sacred about the barefoot bride on the scratched wooden dance floor with her hair coming unpinned and the people she loves all around her. A mysterious glory surrounds the child spinning in circles next to her, giddy to be up past bedtime. The awkward dance moves and ringing laughter can serve as reminders of our humanness.

And there is something so compelling about a Savior who will enter into the middle of it all.

Research shows that 70 percent of young adults will drop out of church. The most common time is between ages seventeen and nineteen.[1] The stereotypical story is that they go off to college and get rowdy. I know this plotline because I lived it. And I can't help but wonder how we can better meet that innate need for freedom and fun within the church. I think we can sometimes intellectualize faith to the point where learning takes the place of living. But we are beings made to dance and eat and offer toasts and stay up too late sometimes. We are not just minds. We are taste and touch and sight and smell and hearing. We want to feel fully alive. This is not worldly or wicked; it is part of our sacred design.

I won't try to say what this looks like for you. I think the specifics likely vary for each of us and for every church. But I do want to whisper this to you: If you sometimes feel a bit bored or restless with religion, it's okay. If you have a longing for more excitement in your faith, then welcome that desire. If you worry you're not serious enough because you like to have fun, then know you're in good company with a Savior who added to the celebration. If you've thought about rebelling, then consider that maybe what you think can be found only *out there* might actually be part of what God wants to offer you *right here*.

Some might say, "But we have to keep a tight rein on everyone or there will be trouble." I have thought a lot about this. Yes, if we embrace more of the freedom God offers, then there may be those who falter in it at times. But here's the thing: a whole loving community will be there to catch them when they do. The alternative is that they walk away from church and struggle alone, where there is no one to hold them accountable or gently pick them back up. Then the tumble might be more than temporary. I like the first option better.

So let's not allow fear to keep us from embracing everything God has for us. When I watch people fully engaged in celebration, there is a humility and self-forgetfulness and childlikeness that I need more of in my life. I am far too respectable and grown-up for my own good sometimes. I think I need answers and assurance, but it might be I just need to take off the shoes that pinch my feet and join in for one more song.

As the reception finally wound down, we began to carry flower arrangements and food to cars outside. I turned to look back at the nearly empty building and an ache almost swept me right off the sidewalk. Suddenly I felt strangely homesick for Jesus and heaven and a wedding feast. Another dance floor. A crowd of people I've called dear and haven't seen for a while. Joy like wine.

We'll be the bride then, all of us, caught up in wonder and toasting our love story with the eternal light everywhere and on everyone like a divine disco ball.

I plan to say, "Oh yeah!" on that day too.

Let's be the *wild joy*
PEOPLE,
the gift embracers,
the life tasters,
the **ones** who know
not only when *to weep*
but also when to dance
and dance and *dance*.

The
ride

Love is the strongest force in the world.
—Corrie ten Boom

MARK AND I MET ON SUNSHINE MOUNTAIN like a cliché that's true. When I first saw him across the room, I thought, *He's too cute to ever talk to me.* But he did. We'd both come to a retreat for a college ministry and although I'd never attended one of their meetings, when my friend mentioned the event, somewhere deep inside I heard, "Go." He had a project due for school and almost didn't come either, but just before midnight on a Friday he walked in the door.

At the end of the two days, I stood at the edge of a beautiful overlook and out of the corner of my eye saw Mark walking my way. I tried to act cool. *Stay calm. Stay calm.* But when he got about ten feet away, he suddenly did a ninety-degree turn and zipped off in the other direction.

What just happened? I asked myself, bewildered. Then it was time to go, and I climbed into my friend's car, where I stared out the window and wondered if I'd ever see him again. The following week when I went to another get-together for this ministry, Mark was there and followed me out the door afterward. I thought they must send the good-looking boys to talk to the new girls as a strategy to recruit more attendees. He asked what I was doing next, and I babbled on about baking brownies while the friend who had come with me watched with raised eyebrows.

Then Mark inquired if I'd like to get coffee with him and a few friends. A man after my own heart. I agreed and we all went to a little place down the road. We talked for two hours while our companions yawned and tried to amuse themselves with napkins and straws. When he walked me to my car, I thought for sure he would ask for my number, but instead he just said an ordinary farewell. *Huh.*

Months later he'd tell me he'd turned away on the cliff because he'd gotten nervous, and he forgot to ask for my number because he was so flustered. I found this entirely endearing.

Since he didn't have my number, Mark decided to look me up in the college email directory. Fortunately, my maiden name is Armstrong, and I was first on the list. He asked me to go for a bike ride with him, but because I rarely checked my email account back then, I didn't get the message for several days. He spent that time wondering and pacing and looking at his inbox.

When I finally did get the email, I said yes. And here's where things get interesting. I'm a girl raised in Texas, where the roads are flat and the hills are few. The last bike ride I'd taken had been on a pink ten-speed Schwinn along straight sidewalks and neatly manicured golf course paths. When Mark picked me up and I saw two bikes on the back of his car with deep ridges in their tires, I understood I might be in trouble. When he drove us to a state park close by and pointed to a map with squiggly, steep trails, I knew I was.

But I liked this boy already and wasn't about to wimp out. So I smiled and put a helmet on my head. I followed him as best I could and tried not to look at his cute behind.

Now let's just clarify that I am not a coordinated woman. I run into my own coffee table. And it has been in the same spot for twelve years. I also don't like to go fast. So whooshing along on a mountain bike over roots and rocks and lumps is not exactly my sweet spot.

Mark and I came to a huge dip in the path. It might have been fifteen feet, but it felt to me like five hundred. Mark was already down it and on the other side before I could even voice a protest. He waved to me encouragingly. Now this is proof of either my insanity or my instant affection for him, because I gritted my teeth, grasped the handlebars until my knuckles turned white, and went down that thing holler-whispering, "Help me, Jesus!" the entire time. I did not die. And he was impressed. Mission accomplished.

I thought afterward that we must surely be close to being done. Oh, but no. We went on and on. And on. At a certain point, Mark disappeared into the trees in front of me and I had no idea how far we were from the parking lot. My legs ached. Sweat streamed down my back. I smelled worse than the skunks I was certain were watching me with their beady, rabid little eyes. I hopped off the bike and began to walk it down the trail, imagining being eaten by a bear at any moment. I might have sniffled a bit. Then a few seconds later I rounded a bend and there was Mark, leaning on his car, grinning and swigging water from a bottle. I wasn't going to be lost in the wilderness forever and ever, amen.

He had only one question: "Do you want to get some pizza?" I nodded. We got married a little less than two years later.

These days I'm not as likely to hop on a bike. I've got the guy, after all. Instead, I let him go with a hardy group who get their thrills from grueling climbs and high-speed chases. This works out well for everyone.

I've lived this kind of story more than once. Jesus also invites us into a life of intimate adventure. I used to picture this as a nice, calm jaunt on a cruiser bike with a wide, cushioned seat. A basket in the front with a plastic daisy, streamers on the handlebars, and polished silver spokes. The wind in my hair, the sun on my face, me smiling and waving to folks on the sidewalk. But I've learned the trail can be twisty, the potholes deep, the ride lengthy. Certain moments I panic, wondering where Jesus is or what's going to happen to me.

I understand this better now because of a conversation I had with Mark about that first mountain-biking outing. I asked him, "Why did you let me be alone on that trail?" He looked at me with a puzzled expression. "I never left you," he said. "I was always right with you. I always knew exactly where you were and where we were going. You just couldn't see that for a little bit."

And this, I'm finding, is what faith and love and trust over a short, long lifetime are like sometimes.

Crazy *sparks*

> I see someone who will fight for me and protect me and love me in spite of all the ways I am still a wreck.
>
> —Melanie Shankle

I AM A BIRTHDAY LOVER. Light the candles. Bring out the chocolate cake. Take me to dinner or throw me a little party. Let me have a day that is not the regular Monday or Wednesday or Sunday—whenever the momentous occasion may fall. I relish the idea of breaking the routine, slipping the mundane like a leash, filling regular old life with tiny flames and too much frosting.

My husband does not share this love of the unusual or special. He's never needed any particular day to be different from another. He's had the same practical haircut his whole life. He buys a certain shirt and when it wears out, he buys another one *exactly like it* as a replacement. He predictably and happily has the chicken parmesan or pad thai every single time. This makes him steady and dependable. Or, as I like to put it, he keeps his feet on the ground so I can have my head in the clouds.

This mostly works for us.

Except that yesterday, on *his* birthday, when I should have been making everything all about him, I instead found myself declaring, "You're driving me crazy!" I have thought these words from time to time. And I'm sure-as-the-sun-will-rise certain he has done the same. But in sixteen years of marriage, I had not said them right out loud.

Before you begin worrying too much about our blessed union, let me tell you that his response to this expulsion of emotion was a grin and whole lot of manly giggling. He thought it was *hilarious*. He has been wed to me long enough to know that those words weren't really about him. When I said, "You're driving me crazy!" I was really saying, "I'm driving myself crazy and you're the closest living being I can pin it on instead." Yes and amen.

Later I sat on the edge of our bed and pondered the source of my poor choice of words (basically, I put myself in grown-up time-out). A podcast I'd recently listened to by Gretchen Rubin popped into my mind. She and her sister had discussed how some of us prefer familiarity and others novelty. Gretchen describes this in her book *Better Than Before*: "I'm definitely in the familiarity camp. I love to reread my favorite books and to watch movies over and over. I eat the same foods, more or less, every day. I like returning to places I've visited before. Other people thrive on doing new things."[1]

When I first heard Gretchen talk about this, it highlighted a difference in my marriage. Mark is a familiarity fan. I am a novelty craver. I still don't even buy the same kind of shampoo *ever* because I like trying something different. My life is full of good things. But it's also full of the *same* things. We've lived in the same town for about fifteen years and the same house about fourteen. We've gone to the same church for over a decade. I write in the same coffee shops and eat at the same restaurants. And this, in so many ways, is such a gift. But for me it's also a challenge.

As a creative thinker, *new* is essential for what I do. I once told Mark that whatever is new or different is like a tree, and after a while it feels like I've picked all the fruit off of it. It's still a wonderful tree, but it doesn't feed me creatively in the same way it did before. Whether I like this or not, it is so.

I had been really looking forward to Mark's birthday because it would be out of the ordinary. He, being tired from a string of stressful events in our lives, pretty much wanted to skip his birthday and have a regular, restful day. Instead of respecting his wishes, I kept trying to force him to have the best and most thrilling time ever. Complete with excitement and fun-fun experiences. And when he didn't enthusiastically comply, I got pouty.

We live in a Jerry Maguire world that thinks love means being able to say, "You complete me." But that's just another way of saying, "I'm expecting you to be the answer to all my unmet needs." As I think back over my marriage to Mark—and it has been a good and happy one—the times when I've felt least satisfied have been the ones when I have demanded he take ownership of something that is really my responsibility.

So I decided my gift to Mark on his birthday would be to take the novelty need off my invisible but ever-present emotional to-do list for him. In search of some help, I went to Gretchen Rubin's website to see what her readers had to say about this issue. I noticed an unexpected theme in the discussion that went like this: *Even what's familiar can be novel.* For example, we can count on a sunrise every morning, but it will never be the same one twice.

It was as if those commenters climbed right into the middle of my marriage to give me an aha moment. I didn't have to choose between familiar and novel. I could begin looking for the novel *within* the familiar.

I have never sat at this particular table in this particular coffee shop on this particular day. And I never will again. I have never celebrated my husband's forty-third birthday—it is a new thing regardless of what we do together on that day. Every moment is a never-before miracle, and it's up to me to have eyes to see it that way. To not assume I recognize it and already know it and therefore it has nothing to offer me.

I will look for other ways to honor my desire for novelty as part of my creative work. Maybe I'll travel more. Or take an online class. Or give myself a bigger budget for books. But I think what I've needed most is to shift my way of thinking so that I can also appreciate more of what's all around me, the divine in the ordinary. My dear husband helps me a lot with this when I don't resist it. And, yes, I help him expand his horizons a bit.

I think this is part of what marriage (or any meaningful relationship) offers us. We are sometimes driven crazy so we may become a bit more sane. "Iron sharpens iron" (Prov. 27:17) sounds quite noble and yet I think it really just means, "Get two people close enough to each other and sparks are gonna fly." Sparks of conflict. Sparks of our differences bumping up against each other. Sparks of *my* way and *your* way. And, yes, hopefully also sparks of passion and warmth and helping each other become the very best version of ourselves.

Sparks like candles all over the frosted cake.

Happy Birthday, Sweetheart.

Ordinary, *divine*

> Bravery can be found in the big moments, but more and more I'm convinced that bravery looks like one million small moments of simply showing up.
>
> —Kaitlyn Bouchillon

I SPENT MOST OF YESTERDAY in the kitchen. This is unusual for me. But there were groceries to put away and there was lunch to make and dinner to prepare for family night when our daughter and her husband come over. As I sliced deep purple eggplant and sautéed brilliant green zucchini and tucked fresh blueberries into a corner of the refrigerator, I felt restless. A small voice inside me kept insisting, "You should be doing something more important."

Then I thought of an episode of *Chef's Table* I'd just watched about Massimo Bottura, owner of the third best restaurant in the world. In one segment of the show, he goes to the place in Modena, Italy, where he gets the Parmigiano Reggiano for his recipes. The cheesemaker, a gray-haired man who has worked there for years, pulls out a wheel with clear delight. He thumps the cheese gently and listens as if to a symphony. Then with great tenderness and practiced swiftness, he splits it down the middle. And in this moment of unveiling, his expression is of an artist beside a completed canvas. It is pride and joy and wonder. It is the way we look when our work is declaring, "This is part of what I was put on earth to do."

I was struck by the extravagance and beauty in this. It is marvelous to think the Creator made a man to make this cheese. And something about being a cheesemaker in love with your calling declares, "I'm not God." It is, somehow, humble and worshipful in a way I can't fully explain but long for in my own life. It reminds me of my favorite passage in *Simply Tuesday* by Emily P. Freeman, where she tells her spiritual director how she made soup on a Sunday.

> I put on music, chopped carrots and celery, boiled chicken and minced garlic. I warmed bread, added heavy dollops of butter on top, opened the windows so I could hear the kids playing in the driveway while I worked in the kitchen, their laughter piercing the sound of the wind through the coloring leaves in the yard.
>
> I did all of that, but all I told Marion was, "I made soup." And just when I realized how dumb that sounded, when I caught myself wanting to explain why making soup was a thing, she said something that surprised me.
>
> "That's beautiful."
>
> And I began to cry.
>
> This simple act of soup means I'm here in this moment, engaging in something I love. Yesterday, making soup was a spiritual act of worship.[1]

As I pondered Emily's words and the inexplicable joy of the cheesemaker, I found the nagging voice within me growing quieter. Instead, I began to say "thank you" right in the middle of my quiet, mundane kitchen. Thank you for the sizzle of the garlic. Thank you for the flavor of the salt. Thank you for rest and loveliness and little things.

I'm not the first one to unexpectedly stumble upon the divine among the common. Brother Lawrence did so in the kitchen of a French monastery over three hundred years ago. Instead of resenting the monotony and smallness of his chores, Brother Lawrence decided to seek God's presence always and in everything. He writes, "Men invent means and methods of coming at God's love, they learn rules and set up devices to remind them of that love, and it seems like a world of trouble to bring oneself into the consciousness of God's presence. Yet it might be so simple. Is it not quicker and easier just to do our common business wholly for the love of him?"[2]

That last phrase calls to me: *our common business wholly for the love of him*. It reminds me of the framed verse Mark and I have in our home office. "Make it your ambition to lead a quiet life" (1 Thess. 4:11). Another translation says "make it your *goal*." However many times I read them, these feel like strange, unfamiliar words. I would fill in the blank differently. Make it your ambition to change the world. Make it your goal to do grand things for God. Make it your aim to be busy and in demand. I am in need of a tender edit.

The Westminster Catechism says, "The chief end of man is to glorify God and enjoy him forever."[3] I can do this in a kitchen alone just as well as I can in front of a crowd. And I find often what I am asking, really, when I'm restless and striving is not, "What will glorify God and how can I enjoy him?" but instead, "How can I be good and prove my worth?" I have noble intentions in this question. Because for so long what I thought God wanted most was for me to behave. But I am learning, slowly learning, that what he really wants is my affection.

This changes everything, because "being good" often translates to doing what is outwardly noticeable or religious. It is the cloak of the Pharisee trying to drape itself around me. But God, I am discovering, is not interested in the show. He can be made much of in the soup bowl and the sliver of cheese and the eggs turned over on a silent morning. In whatever seems ordinary to us in our lives and work. The diapers and the dishes and the note slipped into the mailbox.

Perhaps this is true because it's then that we forget ourselves. We become lost in the little gifts and tiny moments. Then they lead us, like bread crumbs, back to the feet of the Maker of all. "Oh, there you are," we say to him. "This is not where I was expecting to find you." And I think perhaps he smiles and says, "Ah yes, but I've been here all along."

Let's see the *divine*
IN THE ORDINARY,
the **big** in the **small**,
the *meaningful*
in the mundane,
the HOLY in
all things *humble*.

23

All
favorites

> This big world we live in is made up of individual people struggling, trying, growing, living. We are not just a group of anonymous breathing creatures that coexist together, taking up our fair share of oxygen and soil. . . . We are meant to live with our eyes open. And it starts with looking at one person at a time.
>
> —Katie Kenny Phillips

I PULL MY HAIR INTO A MESSY PONYTAIL, swipe gloss across my lips, and grab the first shirt I can reach in the closet. I'm not even sure if my earrings or shoes match my outfit. I'm tired and grumpy and don't care about looking presentable on this particular morning. "It's just a regular day. I'm just going to a coffee shop to work," I tell myself. "I won't see anyone I know anyway."

I make it to the counter and ask for the caffeine-infused beverage I'm hoping will revive me. I add a day-old scone to my order, perhaps feeling pity for it because it looks like me—a little rough around the edges. As I turn to go to my seat, I hear my name. "Holley?" a feminine voice inquires. I look up to see a lovely creature standing in front of me. Shampoo-commercial curls, carefully applied mascara, and the boots I've seen all over the internet as the hot pick of the season. For a moment I consider pretending not to speak English. But before I can hatch an escape plan, she says, "I connected with you at a speaking engagement a couple of years ago."

Alarm bells begin to go off in my mind. *She saw me at a speaking engagement? With my makeup done and my best clothes on? She's probably wondering if I have become homeless since that time.*

I cross my arms and suddenly discover I have something in my teeth. This means I not only appear closed off but also inadvertently make a face at her as I try to dislodge whatever is likely to show itself should I dare to smile. All I can think about is *me, me, me.* And suddenly I hear a deep whisper down in my heart, "She is your assignment right now. She is the person I have put in front of you to love in this moment."

I wish I could say I welcome this with maturity and gladness. That I instantly quote a Scripture passage or recall some tips from the "Three Ways to Be Kind" article I just read. But instead, I do the inner equivalent of hiding in a corner, which means I stand there awkwardly while this perfectly nice person waits for a response.

Then I actually do recall a line I read recently: "God does not show favoritism."[1] I occasionally feel pressure from well-meaning industry experts to "network" and "build relationships with influencers" and "be part of the most relevant tribe," but I've settled into gut-knowing this is not the kingdom way. We are to love and see and treat everyone the same.

But this morning, right here, I realize I am still guilty of another kind of favoritism. In this case, it's that I allow a particular sort of person to have power over me in a way I don't give to others. I'm letting this woman, without her even meaning to, make me feel small and a bit afraid and less-than. I'm familiar with this scenario, and it usually involves the same kind of woman every time. She's beautiful, well-dressed, and charming. She's the one whose lunch table I glanced longingly at in high school. The one who has the magazine-worthy family photos posted all over social media. The kind standing right in front of me with questions in her eyes.

I'm caught off guard as I consider her hopeful expression. And I suddenly understand she might be nervous too. She's likely wondering, *Do you remember me? Are you going to like me? Was I silly to say hello to you?* We're both unsure and vulnerable and perhaps considering bolting for the exit. She'll just be wearing cuter shoes when she does it. I straighten my shoulders, unfold my arms, look her in the eyes, and decide I'm going to try to make her feel like the most important person in the world right now. I give her my full attention, and after a bit I stop wondering if she's noticing my roots in desperate need of a highlight, the stain on my jeans, or the right eyebrow hair that will not, shall not, be tamed.

She tells me how she's a writer too. She asks questions about angst and courage and putting yourself out there. I talk about the journey I've been on, how God took me through a season of go and do and dream to this new one of stay and rest and be. And how it might all be different next year because he is mysterious and untethered, and we are all just riding on the winds with him.

She nods and lets out a breath of relief. We trade numbers and say we'll keep in touch. I finally get to my table and sit down with my coffee and day-old scone. I'm grateful for our brief exchange, and I think about how I could have missed it, how I could have let fear get in the way. I could have played favorites and said, "I'll love on people who make me feel safe but not those who, without even meaning to, could push buttons that make me feel inadequate inside." And the reality is no one has their hands on those buttons but me. I am the manager and engineer and puppet master—the only woman behind the curtain.

We talk a lot these days about loving those who seem to be in need. But we can forget to mention loving those who might tempt us to feel as if we are the ones who are lacking. I see the gorgeous woman in front of me and think she has it all together. I assume I have nothing to give her and she could unintentionally take so much from me. But she is actually falling apart a little in a quiet, unseen corner of her heart. She needs encouragement. She needs help being brave and breath beneath her wings. She needs a fellow traveler on this journey to say, "You really can do this. You're going to be all right."

I think God's secret for not showing favoritism is this: "The LORD does not look at the things people look at. People look at the outward appearance, but the LORD looks at the heart" (1 Sam. 16:7). I want to look beyond my preferences and admirations, my insecurities and assumptions, my appraisals and fears. I want to stop asking, "How does this person see me?" and instead understand, "How can I really see them?" Not the surface but the heart, not the boots but the journeyer, not the shell but the glorious, eternal being on the inside just waiting to be found and known and called worthy.

We are all fragile.

We are all fearful.

We can all pinky swear to each other, "I will look at you as the God-made miracle you are rather than a self-made mirror of who I'm not."

24

Cheeky

I'VE HAD THREE NICKNAMES in my lifetime. The first was "H. E.," short for Holley Ellen. The simple enough explanation for this nickname is that I'm named after my grandfather and people needed a way to distinguish between the two of us or we'd both come running. The second, "Cheese Queen," was set like a tiara on my head in high school by my friend who'd say it as an affectionate rebuke after I chattered on about another nice-smelling boy or an oh-so-romantic movie. The third, "Cheeks," was tossed out by a parade-like variety of people through the years. The reason being as plain as my very own face.

We all have that quality about us that makes us wonder exactly what God was thinking when he bestowed it on us. The hips. The rebellious hair. The birthmark like a coffee stain spilled over our shoulder. Growing up, I leaned into the mirror and pinched my own two cheeks like a nosy relative across the table at Sunday dinner. I wanted to understand them. I wanted to undo them. I wanted to mold them like clay until I had a thin, fine face like a model on a magazine cover.

Those cheeks were my "you can't really be beautiful" card. The one the critical voice inside myself pulled out and read when I stepped too close to believing I was truly lovely. I was allowed to be "cute." And I heard that as a replacement for the adjectives I truly wanted most, like the consolation prize in a contest I would never win. Why couldn't I hear "stunning" or "gorgeous" or "elegant" just once instead?

Beauty was a mold shaped by society with firm lines and deep grooves and my cheeks did not fit. They stuck out and spilled over the edges and caught the sun until they turned an unfortunate shade of red.

One day in college, a girl with perfect waves in her hair and white teeth in her smile and enviable curves in her silhouette walked up to me. She shuffled and stared at the ground before finally squaring her shoulders bravely. "I have something to tell you," she said quite seriously. I nodded and prepared myself for the worst. "I know I'm not supposed to be envious of anyone," she began, "but I really wish I had your cheeks." She said this like a dark, heavy secret she'd carried for a long time. A pebble in her soul that nagged at her until she just had to deal with it, like one of those things you try to get over but can't quite yet. I have no idea what I said in return. If I'd thought fast enough, I might have offered, "I'll trade you for your lips or your eyelashes or your adorable ankles."

I lay in bed that night and stared up at the ceiling. *Huh*, I kept thinking over and over. Her little declaration had been like finding out the sky isn't actually blue or the earth really is as flat as a syrup-soaked pancake. I had no place to store her words, no framework in my mind where they fit. So I set them down in a corner somewhere, and every once in a while I'd look at them just to be sure they were still there, that someone hadn't snatched them away in the night like a bandit. But, no, they stayed.

And somehow their presence began helping me begin to think about beauty differently. The next time I flipped through my family's scrapbook, the one going back for generations, I saw my cheeks on the faces of my mother, grandmother, and great-grandmother. The way I looked wasn't just about me; it was about history. It was part of a long tale of falling in love, white front porch swings, turkey dinners, lullabies, funerals, life and life and life. I liked those cheeks in those photos. They looked to me to be strong and gentle, feminine and welcoming, like a soft place for eyes to land in this brick-hard world.

Years and years later I went to the grocery store with a list in my hand. At the deli counter, I asked for a pound of sweet honey ham and a stack of sharp cheddar cheese. The shy girl working that day kept stealing glances my way as she filled my order. When she handed the plastic sleeve across the counter, she said barely above a whisper, "You have a kind face." *Oh*, I thought, startled and unexpectedly pleased, *it must be the cheeks*.

And as I drove home that day, I started to wonder, very tentatively and slowly, *What if God really did intentionally make me this way? What if beauty isn't just about me or even just about history but is about right here, right now too? What if this is the face I most need for what God has for me to do?* I thought of this when teary-eyed counseling clients stepped into my office and felt instantly comfortable in my presence. I remembered it at conferences where I worried about not looking "cool" but found that what folks really needed, because they were scared just like me, was someone who looked *warm*.

We are works of art who can say to God, "You knit me together in my mother's womb" (Ps. 139:13). And perhaps if we had been witnesses of our own creation, we might have seen that what we think should have been left out is actually the crowning touch. "Ah yes, the cheeks," God could have said with a smile. Or whatever you question about your shape and form. Maybe we have defined beauty all wrong. Because I have known many artists, and when a piece has what it needs to fulfill their vision for it, they stand back and say, "Beautiful." And it doesn't matter a bit to them if anyone else agrees. The artist gets the final word.

If that is so, then I want to see differently. Not with the eyes of the beer commercials and the touched-up lingerie photos and the stilettos on runways. I want to look at who I am, at all of me, and glimpse every cell and strand as a wonder and mystery, as part of God's infinite, incomprehensible doing. I want to do that now and also later when the years dim my eyes. When I can hardly make out the shape of my wrinkled face in the mirror, when I pinch those cheeks with trembling hands as I still say it to myself and all my sisters:

I am beautiful.

You are beautiful.

We are beautiful.

This has always been true; we just didn't always know it.

Get a
hanky

> I believe in some blending of hope and sunshine sweetening the worst lots. I believe that this life is not all; neither the beginning nor the end. I believe while I tremble; I trust while I weep.
>
> —Charlotte Brontë

I AM NOT A GRACEFUL CRIER. No dainty dabbing at flawless waterproof mascara above flushed, feminine cheeks. I am, instead, an awkward resister of tears. I squinch my eyes while the drops leak slowly as if from a bad faucet. In audacious contrast, my nose gushes like a red fire hydrant and turns approximately that shade. I always get a headache and hardly ever feel better. I just get mad about my nose running because I'm invariably without a hanky or even tissues and have to use my sleeve (or help us all, my pant leg) when no one is looking.

Because of all this, I don't cry often. No moist eyes while watching touching commercials. The books on my shelf are bereft of those little round watermarks on the heartbreaker pages. And I've considered discreetly sprinkling a bit of water on my cheeks during beautiful wedding toasts just to fit in with the crowd.

I'm also a licensed counselor, so a lot of the crying has been trained right out of me. Folks don't tend to want the professional response to be, "Oh my goodness, that is just the worst thing I've ever heard!" followed by unsightly weeping. This is not behavior generally considered worth paying for by the hour.

If I was my own counselor, I would have adequate reason to fire myself for offenses today. For example, when I started crying in the car this morning, I responded only with an uncompassionate eye roll and the thought, *Seriously? I do not have time for this.* With ten minutes to go before I pulled into the parking lot, I was not interested in whatever my soul was trying to bring to the surface. It was Monday. I had work to do. Guests were arriving at our house later. *Thou shalt calm thyself down.*

It took only about three seconds to figure out where the tears were coming from and then, unfortunately, it got worse. *Blast—* now I'm going to have to write about that, aren't I? Then I will probably cry right here in the coffee shop where I'm writing, and people will think I'm having a breakdown or watching YouTube videos with kittens in them. I'm certain the barista already thinks I'm here so often because I don't have a job. When she asks what I'm working on and I say, "A book," she gives me the look—the one that says, "I'm sure your mama will love it, honey." But I digress. And I'm procrastinating. Because here's the thing—my dog is sick. (If you're not a dog person, please humor me a little for just a few paragraphs. There's a grander point coming, I promise.)

Our hound is a beagle-basset mix (aka "bagel"), and we got her from an animal shelter when she was just a little more than a year old. Actually, I found her on petfinder.com first. She was the "featured pet," and I fell in love with her immediately. We were leaving the next day for vacation, so I drove almost two hours and one state over to put down a ten-dollar deposit on her. She was in an outdoor pen with a whole bunch of bigger, scarier dogs. She stood in the center of that intimidating circle and wagged her tail happily. I thought I could learn a thing or two from that kind of thinking.

We picked her up a week later, and she was so startled she shook the whole way home while I held her on my lap. When we gave her a bath later, something clicked in her mind and she ran in giddy circles around our house until flopping spread-eagle on the floor, *her floor.*

That was about fourteen years ago—go ahead and do the math. Katie (aka "the Beast") is over a hundred or a zillion in dog years. I'm not entirely sure because the whole dog years = people years equation keeps changing. But the bottom line is that she's as ancient as the hills now.

We've watched her little black and white face turn gray around the eyes. She lets the squirrels stroll by instead of chasing them down with an intensity contrary to the rest of her temperament. She sleeps like it's an Olympic sport and walks like she's got all the time in the world. Only it looks like she doesn't. And I just about cannot stand it.

The Beast has vestibular disease and just had another episode. It makes her sway like a drunk down the hallway, and if it weren't so dang unfortunate, it would be quite funny. We took her to our vet, who basically said, "She's old, you know." And we said, "Yes, but we are quite skilled in denial, thanks." She could have a lot more life in her. For all I know, when I get home she'll be licking the kitchen tile (her new favorite pastime) and swinging her tail like a helicopter propeller as she has done all her days. *But I don't know that anymore.* And it's the not knowing that is so painful.

In grad school, I studied the different kinds of losses. I'm sure I memorized them all at some point to pass a test, but I can only remember one right now. I even remember the multiple choice question about it: "Which type of loss is the most difficult to treat?" Answer: C (ambiguous loss). An ambiguous loss is one that is not entirely clear. Perhaps it might not even happen—or at least not yet. It's not necessarily the *saddest* kind of loss. It just poses unique challenges because it offers no closure, only wondering and some confusion. Uncertainty makes a fine mess of the usual grieving process.

But isn't all of life really one big story of ambiguous loss in a way? The hello is a preview to the goodbye. The start is the beginning of the finish. The forming of the bond is a sure sign that there will be the pain of parting at some point. We live smack in between birth and death every single day. There is no other way. And we, frail creatures, want resolution. We want the knowing. Please tell me the facts and the exact future so that I can deal with them. But this is not the way of the heart. What the heart needs to know is that we will be okay anyway. And this is the impossible, inexplicable promise of Jesus—*we will*.

While I'm reassured by and oh so grateful for this, I wish it also meant we would not still cry in the car. Or beside the hospital bed. Or while we stare at the phone and hope to hear something, *anything*. Or when we start packing up the desk just in case the rumors are true. Even when the summer sky is so gorgeous it hurts to look at it because our souls have gotten themselves homesick all of a sudden.

And, yes, also when we rub the silly old hound belly and count her smelly breaths while she tail-thumps the carpet like a contented, uncoordinated drummer.

This is the root of the fear and why I resist the tears: I want to be in control. And I sure don't ever want to let go. But the truth is I've never had my hands on the hinges of the universe. When I'm at my bravest, I wrestle my way to accepting this and even embrace it on occasion. Because I've come to see that the door of change swings both ways, grief on one side and joy on the other. We can't have one without the other. That's just not the deal. And not liking it doesn't make it untrue. If we dare to love at all, this life is just a whole lot of coming and going, happy and hard, with tears as the familiar butlers in the foyer.

fiercehearted

It occurs to me as I'm writing this that there comes a day in every person's life when the time has come to get ourselves a proper hanky. To take hold of it like our own brave little flag of surrender to the beauty and the ashes. To finally stop saying things like, "This is nothing compared to what others are facing" or "Really, I'm fine" or "Let's not get too caught up in the moment." To just let the crying do its God-given work without any further resistance or reprimand.

I think, entirely unexpectedly, this is mine.

26

emotional Duct Tape

Courage does not always roar, sometimes it is a quiet voice at the end of the day that says, "I will try again tomorrow."

—Mary Anne Radmacher

FOLKS HAVE SAID A CERTAIN PHRASE to me almost all my life, and to this day it always makes me look over my shoulder to see if they're talking to someone else. Every once in a while someone will just drop it right into a conversation: "You look like you have it all together."

They might as well be saying, "You seem like you do the pole vaulting event in the Olympics" or "You seem like you play defense for the Dallas Cowboys." In my mind, this observation has no correlation to reality or rational thinking. I immediately wonder if the person saying it is on drugs or perhaps recently sustained some sort of head injury. My initial instinct is to ask them to count backward slowly from ten so I can decide if I need to call the paramedics.

Someone first said this to me at a youth retreat when I was smack in the middle of the awkward teen years. Our little group had gathered around a campfire for s'mores and soul baring. The leader asked us to share something encouraging about someone else. An older, more popular girl (who, ironically, was never particularly nice to me) said *those* words. "Holley seems like she has it all together." I almost choked on my marshmallow.

Then more recently an email made its way to my inbox that said something like, "Holley seems to balance it all. I want to know her secret." I should have let my hubby handle that one—he would have *plenty* of secrets to share with the class. An astounding case could be made for my not-togetherness based on our first year of marriage alone—including a certain incident involving cinnamon rolls that refused to rise, me bawling on the kitchen floor, and a hasty stop at the donut shop on the way to Sunday school.

After hearing this phrase so inaccurately for so long, I've decided the time has come to officially and publicly set the record straight.

I'm especially feeling that way this morning because I have just wrapped up a two-week stretch of wildness and chaos. Major life events, visits, travel, moves, graduations, sick dog, work deadlines, empty refrigerator shelves—the works. I survived and did not kill anyone. This seems like a victory.

But here's the thing: as I've already shared, I've struggled with anxiety throughout my life. I keep it in check via a complex system I have built through the years. I need eight hours of sleep. I can't eat too much sugar, dairy, or gluten. I have to exercise most days or my serotonin levels drop and depression starts beating on my door like a vacuum cleaner salesman. I require at least a few moments of quiet and space to think or my brain begins darting about like a rabid squirrel. If I ever appear to have it together, then it is because I have invented my own strange sort of emotional duct tape to wrap around my days.

This is a perilous situation, and when life goes sideways, the duct tape is toast. All bets are off, and pretty soon I'm battling in a straight-up war against the crazy. My four biggest anxiety enemies (shame, guilt, perfectionism, and fear) run amuck and wreak havoc without restraint. While their voices are frequently present as little whispers in the back of my mind, when I'm stressed out, they become a roar. Just this morning, for example, I was harassed and taunted . . .

Shame: You didn't talk enough to your relatives last weekend while you were visiting them. If you really loved people, if you really were a *good* Christian, then instead of going to bed early, you would have stayed up with them. Selfish-shmellfish.

Guilt: Yes, and someday they won't be around anymore. Then you will look back and think, *Why didn't I try harder? Why didn't I do more?* Then you will boo-hoo like a widdle bitty baby. Wah-wah.

Perfectionism: (rolls eyes) Puh-leaze. Forget those two. We need to make a plan. Get out a list and a calendar. Better yet, get a calculator. We will figure out the exact amount of words per hour you need to speak when you're with other people. Snap to it, sister.

Fear: Focus, everyone! I'm trying to make breakfast here. These eggs probably have salmonella in them. This spinach could be covered in pesticides. Your husband is eating BACON. Don't you remember the article we read about the evils of processed meat? We are all going to DIE RIGHT NOW. (Hits panic button and internal sirens and flashing lights commence.) *Danger. Danger. Danger.*

This, on many days, is my world. Times a hundred. So the reality is while someone is standing there saying, "You have it all together," and I am sweetly smiling back at them or offering a thank-you, what's going on inside my head is utter mutiny. Shame declares, "Fraud. Fraud. Fraud." Guilt hollers, "Oh really? Just tell them what you did last week." Perfectionism insists, "Those words *could* be true if you'd just do what I say." Fear mutters, "Person. Person. You are talking to a PERSON. Scary. Scary. Scary. Middle school lunchroom. Junior high locker room. High school prom. We are all going to DIE RIGHT NOW."

When this happens, I try to silence the voices in very spiritual ways, like eating a hot fudge sundae, including the eerily and artificially red maraschino cherry (which makes fear faint). Or scrolling through social media and telling myself everyone else has it all together in their fabulous, cool lives (plenty of material for shame and guilt). Or compulsively cleaning my house, because the more out of control I feel the more controlling I act (score one for perfectionism).

Then eventually I have this moment when I finally tell shame and guilt and perfectionism and fear, "You are not the boss of me." And I remember Jesus is instead. So I ask him for help or text a friend who knows all the variations of my crazy and request that she please remind me of what's true. I manage a few deep breaths and set the spoon down. I go for a walk. I take a nap. I sit on the back porch. Slowly, slowly the shift happens. I feel a little better. I believe I'm going to make it and that I'm not a truly terrible person after all.

I used to think I would get to the place where shame and guilt and perfectionism and fear would totally disappear. I thought I could become holy moley enough to eradicate them completely. But I've come to believe life doesn't work that way. Instead, every time I don't totally give in it's like throwing a bucket of shrinking potion on them. I imagine one day they'll be squeaky little mice instead of giant, hairy bully monsters. And I hope instead that love and grace and peace and courage will get bigger and be what I hear first and most often.

Here's what I know in this moment: sometimes it's inconvenient and annoying and downright exasperating to be human. But it's what we've got to work with. So perhaps one favor we can do for each other is to not believe anyone has it all together and instead recognize we're each just trying to hold it together the best we can. In other words, we all need even more kindness than it seems. And to borrow each other's duct tape sometimes.

Let's make this
our declaration:
instead of trying to
have it ALL TOGETHER,
we will *dare* to do
real, messy, imperfect
life all *together*.

27

pedicures, Mice, Therapy

> In some ways I am brave, but it feels a lot more like Full Of Fear than FearLess. And it looks a lot more like uncertainty and hormones than self-assured and self-controlled.
>
> —Katie Kump

I LOVE COUNSELING the way some women love manicures and pedicures. Yes, please, give me the comfy couch of a counselor over the salon chair anytime. When I say this out loud in public, the folks around me tend to widen their eyes and blink very quickly as if they're afraid I may suggest group therapy as our next girls' night out. When I ask about this response, I often hear, "Counseling just seems so scary." This has happened often enough that I think it's worth a conversation and a few confessions here.

Counseling usually seems frightening because people tend to assume the counselor is going to think they're nuts. And it's true that walking into a room and immediately confessing your deepest struggles to a stranger is risky behavior under basically any other circumstance, particularly office Christmas parties. But, fortunately, because I've been one and known many, I can testify counselors almost universally think highly of their clients and learn far more from them than the other way around.

Every client I saw, whether she struggled with depression or drug addiction or found herself in the middle of an affair, taught me something new. I saw each one as strong and brave and beautiful. Not because she was flawless (none of us are) but because she had the courage to say, "I want things to be different. And I'm willing to ask for help." Of all the words we can utter, these are some of the fiercest. We all have at least that *one thing* that seems to beat us every time. But not all of us have the guts to get to the place where we're willing to stare it down and go as many rounds as it takes to overcome it. This is worthy of respect and applause in my world.

Because we know folks tend to feel nervous when they come to see us, counselors work hard to have reassuring responses—right down to our facial expressions. In general we're not supposed to drop our jaws or burst into tears or drift off to sleep. We can be like Vegas poker players, except with the occasional affirming head nod. I've found this is especially important in the middle of intense, highly emotional confessions.

In one such moment with a client I was doing quite well. I felt empathetic and deeply engaged with what she was saying. Then all of a sudden, out of the corner of my eye, I saw a flash of gray streak across the carpet. I apparently looked uncharacteristically startled and unnerved. I watched my client evaluate this unexpected reaction. She finally cleared her throat and carried on, but only a few seconds later the little gray blur struck again. This time it slowed long enough for me to come to a no-doubt-about-it conclusion. There was a mouse. Right. Under. My. Client.

I mentally ran through every lecture I'd heard in grad school. I thought of all the textbooks I'd read. I racked my brain for even a tiny bit of knowledge that might apply to this situation. Nope, not a single sentence had prepared me for the "wildlife encounter" scenario. I tried to quickly consider the implications. My client could have a panic attack. This could lead to PTSD. She might go home and swig gallons of whiskey straight out of the bottle. Or catch the next flight to mouse-free Antarctica, never to return. Better not to say a word. Unfortunately, my wavering facade had already failed. My client looked at me, raised an eyebrow, and asked, "What's going on?"

Because counselors have a somewhat annoying tendency to answer questions with more questions, I responded, "So are you afraid of mice?" In less time than it took to say yes, she planted both feet on that couch as if the floor were a blazing fire and wrapped her arms around her chest like a bulletproof vest. I had my answer.

Under normal circumstances I would have joined her and then hollered until someone came to rescue us both from our cushion-covered barricade against imminent destruction. Instead, I forced myself to slowly and reasonably inquire, "Would you like to go to another room?" She vigorously nodded and I leaped for the door, threw it open, and we hopped into the next space as if we were walking on hot coals. Because surely if we had even touched the ground, that rascal would have been on our ankles like a rottweiler.

We settled in again with our hearts pounding, feeling a new and deeper sense of appreciation for life and each other after such a harrowing experience. I asked her to continue the important thought so rudely interrupted and leaned in to listen. I sensed a big breakthrough coming. But then—a flicker of movement by the door. That brazen creature popped up in front of us again like a miniature banshee. We both screamed, which proved to be quite effective. Our intruder immediately and permanently retreated back under the door.

My client and I turned to each other and did the only thing we could. We laughed and laughed and laughed. And then we carried on. I don't remember exactly what we said after all the mayhem, but I do recall how that experience became part of what was to be a remarkable transformation in that woman's life.

Dr. Henry Cloud, a psychologist and author, describes how one of his professors told a fervent class of students he was going to reveal the one factor research had proven truly helps clients. Cloud could hardly contain his anticipation; at last, the formula that could cure everything and everyone. He shares what happened next in his book *The Power of the Other*:

> I sat eagerly, waiting to find out the secret of helping people. Here, at last, I would learn that esoteric kernel of wisdom that I had been seeking all of this time. The professor looked at us and said, "It's the relationship. What actually brings about change in people, and the cure, is the relationship between the psychologist and the client," he explained.[1]

It turns out counseling is not really about fancy terms or techniques. Approximately 80 percent of counseling is simply not facing the mouse alone. In other words, "Two are better than one" (Eccles. 4:9). Who knows, had I not been present when the mouse appeared, my client might be perched on the couch to this day. Or at least she might have stayed there for a few more hours. Because this is how we all can live—stuck and overwhelmed by something we've given much more power than it actually possesses or deserves.

I thought of this last fall when I found myself on the other side of counseling. I'd been fleeing the same mouse for months in my life. I knew it would not devour me, but it sure *felt* like it could. And that it wanted to. With extra mustard and a side of fries. So I started going to counseling again.

Yes, I have friends and family members to process life with as well, and I'm so grateful for all of them. But for about a zillion reasons, including objectivity and intentional time and how our brains respond to certain kinds of interactions, talking to them isn't a replacement for counseling. I also believe we need to let the people we love be the people we love. Just like we need to go to the doctor instead of our cousin Rita when we break a leg, even if she is pretty good at making casts out of tree limbs and old rubber bands.

I no longer work as a counselor, and sometimes I miss it. But I plan to go to counseling as many times as I need to for the rest of my life. So if you're looking for a business idea, I'll let you have mine. Start a spa where you get a counseling session and a pedicure at the same time. Then call me, because I am *so* there. In this world that mouse is coming back sooner or later—might as well have our courage up and toenails painted for the next time we jump on the couch.

brave,
Hard Thing

Often the hardest person to fight for is . . . yourself.
But you must. Your heart is needed. You must be
present and engaged in order to love well and fight
on behalf of others. Without you, much will be lost.

—Stasi Eldredge

I DID A BRAVE, HARD THING TODAY. And so, in celebration, I got a sweet and spicy mango habanero taco and a side of sticky, salty cilantro rice from one of my favorite local places. I ate both with a white plastic fork in self-satisfied triumph, sitting especially tall in the driver's seat of my car. I might have even waved that little utensil around like a sword or a victory flag. Because it's that kind of day.

And because this is *the law* in my world. If you do a brave, hard thing for yourself, then you get a treat. I tell this to my friends who are facing their yearly appointments. (If you're in stirrups and you're not a cowgirl, then you deserve at least a cupcake. I'm just sayin'.) I declare it to the scared mamas leaving their babies with a relative or friend or gum-chewing babysitter for the first time. I whisper it in the ears of the dreamers who are walking toward an open door but still shaking in their high-heeled boots with every staccato step.

We, as women, don't need extra motivation to help others. We will sling the stone at the giant or stay up until midnight working on the red ketchup-filled volcano for the science project or stop a semitruck with our pinky finger when it's barreling toward someone we love. But we don't do this as readily for *ourselves*. We have a thousand reasons why. Some are truly selfless. Others are simply because we're frightened. They all get in the way. So when we manage to hop across those obstacles like a field of slick boulders and do the brave, hard thing anyway, well, then it's taco time.

Some folks might say we shouldn't need or want reinforcement for such deeds. We should be inherently and internally motivated. We ought to have a spiritual and supernatural desire that supersedes all this sort of silliness. To them I say, "If you're not going to eat that salsa, can I have it?" I believe God gave us good gifts—including treats—and as long as we're not abusing them, then we're to have at it with joy and gratitude and extra napkins.

The brave, hard thing I did today first involved making a phone call to a stranger. I dislike talking on the phone and try to avoid it the way some people attempt to circumvent raisins in a cookie that would otherwise be quite nice. When someone actually answered, I had to ask for an appointment and give my birthday and tell her *why* I wanted to come in. I managed to say, "I've been experiencing some depression-like symptoms again and my counselor recommended that I talk to a doctor." This is the truth, but there's so much more behind it. Like the fact that my counselor recommended I make an appointment a while ago, but I ignored this advice and watched Netflix and bought yoga pants instead. I didn't mention all this to the receptionist. She put me down for 9:40.

I finished breakfast and hastily got dressed. I imagined the receptionist's thoughts when I arrived at the doctor's office. *Black T-shirt, unwashed hair, lots of blinking—doesn't seem like the measles or mammogram. Must be the depression one.* I waited for an hour in a big room with old magazines and a stack of toys surely infected by the plague. I half-listened to newscasters talk about politics and watermelon carving. I read a bit of a book on my Kindle, which I carry around the way some small children do a security blanket.

Then my name was called and I followed a nurse to a smaller room with crackly paper on the exam table. I thought hard then about going home, about just getting up and walking out, about forgetting this ever happened. Because I didn't want to talk about my depression. I didn't want to ask for help. I wanted to *fix it myself.* Mostly, I didn't want anyone to know I'd already tried to do so and being here was proof that it didn't work out. But right then I looked down at my book again and the words of my friend and fellow writer Jennifer Dukes Lee put their arms around my shoulder:

> Women in particular work hard to hold up defenses. We disguise what we think is wrong about us. We try hard to keep it all together because we are afraid of rejection. But those things that we believe are actually "wrong" about us actually make us approachable to every other woman who is struggling with her own set of wrongs.[1]

I realized how silly it was of me to be afraid to tell a doctor that I was not feeling well. That's why she was there. It's the same with Jesus, who said, "Healthy people don't need a doctor—sick people do. I have come to call not those who think they are righteous, but those who know they are sinners" (Mark 2:17 NLT). He treats not only sin but also all the brokenness that comes from being a human in the world. The kind in our bodies and our hearts. The kind in my brain. He does it in a variety of ways that range from the miraculous to the seemingly mundane. But before we can find healing, we have to say what hurts. To him and to others.

Eventually the door opened and a woman with short blonde hair and eyeglasses perched on her nose came in and sat across from me. She asked questions with kind eyes and made a few notes. I told her about the medicine my counselor recommended and she agreed. She asked for my pharmacy, gave me some instructions, and then said, "I hope this works for you," as she walked out the door.

Side note: I want to quickly clarify what she meant by that because medicine for depression is so often misunderstood. It's not intended to make sure you never feel down. It's to realign your brain so the emotions you feel are more appropriate. If I receive difficult news, then I want to feel fittingly sad. If I'm having a happy day, then I want the capacity to feel joy. When it works well, this medicine is like fixing a thermometer. The readings (emotions) correspond to the actual temperature again. The short story is my brain does not do this well on its own.

After the appointment I breathed a sigh of relief because I was done. I called my husband to share the good news that we had a plan, and I could hear the relieved smile in his voice. Then I drove to the taco shop and got my lunch.

Brave, hard thing. Check-check.

And I am doing another brave, hard thing now. I am telling you this happened. I am not doing so a few decades later when it would feel much safer or while standing on a stage giving a testimony after the depressionish thing has been fully defeated. Instead, I'm saying it only a few moments after, when it is still tender and I want to protect it.

I am writing about this because you might have a brave, hard thing to do too. It's been waiting, calling your name. You have wrestled with it in the dark. You have wondered what people will think. You have tried to do everything *but that*. If so, I want you to know I believe you really can do it. You can make the call. Or face the foe. Or do something that feels entirely too practical and not at all spiritual but is actually God's provision for you—like I believe medicine is for me right now.

What I am trying to say is that *we are worth fighting for too.* God loves all his kids alike. It's only us who differentiate. Who tell ourselves that everyone and everything else is deserving of our courage and compassion and fierceness but us. This is one of the trickiest lies. Please don't believe it. We need you to be strong on your own behalf when necessary. Ask yourself, "What would I do if it was not me but someone I love who was feeling this way, who was in this battle?"

I would have driven anyone else in my life to the doctor today. I would have sat with her in the waiting room and told her I was proud of her for coming. Afterward I would have bought her that mango habanero taco and the lime cilantro rice. I would have thought how these were such small things for such a big victory. I would have smiled and been so glad she'd found something that might be just what she needs I would have thanked God for her courageous, lovely self who had the guts to speak the truth and take the gift of help.

That's what I would have done for you. Absolutely.

So that's what I did for me.

29

different Kind of Sad

> God deliberately chooses imperfect vessels—those who have been wounded, those with physical or emotional limitations. Then he prepares them to serve and sends them out with their weakness still in evidence, so that his strength can be made perfect in that weakness.
>
> —Christine Caine

FOR A LONG TIME I didn't know I was battling depression. And, as with any unknown enemy, this made it harder to fight. When I pictured depression, I thought of not being able to get out of bed in the morning. I thought of entirely gray days filled with tears like raindrops. I imagined not being able to work or pick up the phone or even manage to take a shower. And I felt deep empathy for folks who faced all this. But because my experience felt different, I didn't think I had the right to really claim membership in the same tribe.

Then recently I learned about dysthymia (also known as persistent depressive disorder). It is a milder, chronic form of depression. This is what I have. If major depression is the flu, then dysthymia is that annoying, drawn-out cold you just can't shake. It's likely you're still able to make breakfast and get the kids out the door to school, show up at your desk and finish the project, or put on a brave face for a couple of hours at the birthday party. But inside you're often longing to nap with a comfy blanket on the couch for, oh, about a year.

In other words, you're present in your own life but not fully there—you're not really *you*. At least the best version of yourself. The one who really engages with others and laughs at jokes and gets excited about new ideas. There are many reasons for this but it often simply comes down to one: dysthymia flare-ups make you feel tired. A lot. And it's the sort of weariness that doesn't go away. You might sleep too little. Or too much. But either way, getting through the day can feel like walking in mud. You have to *make* yourself do things—even things you used to really enjoy. Unlike with major depression, you somehow get them done most of the time. But it's like eating food when you've lost your sense of taste and texture. All function and no pleasure. On the days when my dysthymia is worst it's like I'm wearing a raincoat and even if joy is coming down right on top of me, I can't feel it; it just can't soak into my bones.

Dysthymia is also a trickster. It turns your mind into something like the fun house full of mirrors at a carnival. Your thoughts aren't entirely unrelated to reality, but they're distorted. One mistake makes it appear like you're a total failure. A single harsh word has you convinced you're an awful person. All your fine efforts to please God seem as though they have only made him angrier. This is disorienting and startling and scary because while all this is false, it *feels* real. In the shiny, hard surfaces of your mind, it even *looks* real. And often people, with the best of intentions, can say things to you that make it even *sound* real.

"You just need to trust Jesus more," they say.

"Maybe if you ran a marathon every afternoon it would help," they offer.

"Oh, that's just silly" or "Stop being so emotional," they say.

Such comments only bring more shame and guilt, which are already the BFFs of dysthymia and depression. When someone we love is trapped in the fun house, they need heaps of compassion and support. We may look at their lives and pinpoint things they could change. We might even be absolutely right. But here's the thing: they see even more of what's wrong (both real and imagined) than we do. Right now they are handling all they can. They are in the middle of a fight that is deeper and darker and harder than it appears. They are lonely and exhausted and already convinced they should be doing infinitely more and better.

What they need is someone to come along and help them hold up their sword. To acknowledge they're doing the best they're capable of in this moment. To whisper in their ear, "You're an overcomer. You're loved. You're going to *win*. Keep fighting, brave and beautiful soul."

This will encourage and strengthen them. It may also make them realize what they really need to, and that is they are in an actual battle. Because dysthymia can last not just for days or weeks but *years,* those of us facing it can see it as normal. We can believe it's like this for everyone. And this leads to a sort of unfortunate surrender—an acceptance that this is the way life is or simply the way we are. I lived like this for quite a while, with some stretches better than others. Only recently have I really come to understand I have an illness—a chronic one—and that while it is not unbearable, it's also not something I have to give myself over to without question or protest.

Realizing what I face is an actual, physical thing and not a moral failing has been a tremendous relief. I say to myself often these days, "It's not your fault." Yes, it is my responsibility. Just as it is the responsibility of someone with diabetes to watch what they eat and take their medicine. But it's not a failure on my part that I have this condition. It's simply a medical reality. Because of research and brain scans and all kinds of wonderful things, doctors now know this for sure.

So I am following a plan to deal with dysthymia. I'm talking with a counselor. I'm eating well and exercising often. I'm working with a doctor. I'm being intentional about time with positive people. I'm sticking close to Jesus. Because all of this is part of victory in the battle: my body, mind, heart, and soul.

Sometimes I feel disappointed and frustrated that I have to fight so hard. But I am coming to accept my condition. We all have our thorns in the flesh, don't we? Dysthymia is not something I can eliminate completely. But I don't have to let it be the boss of me. I don't have to be defeated by it. I don't have to listen to its voice or do its bidding. And I am proud of myself for what I have accomplished in spite of it.

My situation could have gone differently. I could have given up or given in. Maybe you could have too. Or perhaps someone you love could have. But we are here. We may have bruises. We may have a few scars. But we are still standing. We are mightier than we know, more courageous than we feel, and we belong to a God who has promised all this is temporary. Someday the war will be over, the tears will be wiped away, and we will be strong forever.

If you struggle with dysthymia or depression too, then be gentle with yourself. You have enough enemies to fight without adding yourself to the list. If someone you love struggles with it, then hug them and tell them they are doing better than they know. If you've said hurtful, discouraging things even in the name of love or their best interest, then also tell them you're sorry and you didn't understand. If you've read this and thought, *Huh, what Holley is describing sounds a lot like my life,* then go talk to a counselor or a doctor to find out more. There's power in the knowing.

As the saying goes, "Be kind, for everyone you meet is fighting a hard battle." This happens to be mine. I know my enemy's name now. And I am not afraid to say it out loud. Whatever you're facing today, you don't need to hide or hang your head either.

There is no shame in being a warrior.

Fight on.

Showing Up

You thought you couldn't be Super girl and Captain Awkward at the same time. But I'm thinking we can be both, and together we get the privilege of taking turns and showing up for our people.

—Jennifer Renee Watson

I LOOK AT THE FOUR LOVELY FACES around me and my tummy does a nervous little flutter. I met these women when I spoke to a crowd of more than six thousand. After finding out some of the ladies who attended actually live in my town, I asked them, "Why don't we meet up for real-life coffee?"

I ran late on the way to our get-together. I let my hair blow dry by leaving the windows down in my car. I tried to order a breakfast sandwich and was told, "Um, it's eleven." I wanted to reply, "I promise I've been up for a while. I just like eggs," but I didn't have the guts.

Then I sat down at the table, straightened my jewelry, and fidgeted a bit. Eventually I decided I'd better just come out with it, so I took a deep breath and confessed, "I'm afraid you won't like me as much close up."

You see, it's easy to look good from a distance. Especially when you've had a chance to write out every word you're going to say. And someone has kindly and beautifully accessorized you. And the lights are pretty and the decorations are fabulous and every detail is all so wonderfully in place for you. *What if I disappointed these women when they met just plain ol' me?*

Of course, my fears were unfounded. Everyone was gracious and kind and funny and lovely and didn't mind my windblown hair or messy heart. *Whew.*

As I drove home, I thought about how the worry I expressed is something we all seem to share as women in one way or another. *We all feel more comfortable with a little distance between ourselves and those around us because we're afraid we won't be loved if we're seen close up.*

We might create that distance by saying "I'm fine" when we feel broken inside, holding on to our couch like it's a lifeboat every evening, working too much, drinking too much, doing anything that will make us feel like we can avoid others seeing us as we really are.

But that's not how we're made to live. We need to walk off the stage, out the door, across the room, and spill what's really going on in our lives. We need to let people see our faces without makeup and our souls without scripts and our lives without the polish and practice.

I actually ought to have known this from experience, because I did something crazy at the event where I first met these four women. The evening after I spoke in the big arena, I went upstairs, took off my makeup, pulled my hair into a disheveled ponytail, and changed into some workout clothes that double as pajamas. When I laid my head on the pillow, it seemed God whispered to my heart, "You need to go back down to the lobby."

I thought, *Okay, I'll get dressed again, put on my makeup, and go.* But I felt strongly I was supposed to go as I was. I resisted at first but couldn't shake it, so I finally got up. My husband asked, "Where are you going?" And I said, "I'm heading to the lobby in my pajamas." He rolled over and went back to sleep. I think this nonchalance says something about the amount of abnormal happenings in our marriage.

When I got downstairs, little groups of cute, appropriately clothed women were hanging out. Someone asked, "Are you going to work out?" and I said, "No, these are my pajamas." Then the question came. "Oh, can we take a picture with you?" I shrugged my shoulders and replied, "Sure!" Guess which photos ended up on the internet?

When I finally went back to my room, I felt so much lighter. I realized the reason I needed to go downstairs was to remember I'm not created for a stage. I'm not created to be "on" all the time. Neither are you. Yes, there are days meant for wearing the beautiful dress, adding the extra coat of mascara, and putting our "best" forward. But there are days meant for inviting people into our worst as well. And most of all, there are moments for sharing everything that's in between. In other words, *plain ol' lovely, ordinary, extraordinary you.*

Right before I stepped onto that huge stage earlier in the day, a single declaration of truth came to my heart: "You're not here to impress them. You're here to bless them." Those words let me breathe a sigh of relief because they put everything into perspective again. I wasn't there to show off but to serve. I wasn't speaking to make people like me but to point them to the Savior who loves us all. I hadn't come with an entourage but with encouragement. I didn't need to prove I was better than someone else; I only needed to remind us all that we're more alike than we sometimes realize. We're all a bit afraid. We all want to belong. We all worry we will be too much or not enough.

So let's be brave today. Let's love and be loved. Let's look with gentler eyes at ourselves and each another. Whether we're in pajamas or high-heeled pumps. Whether we're holding a micro-phone or warming up leftover coffee in the microwave as syrup-splattered toddlers run circles around our ankles. Whether we're close up or far away.

None of us needs to have it together; we only need to remember we're better together.

On Ragamuffins

I do not feel like I have the courage for this journey, but I have Jesus—and He will provide. He has given me so much to be grateful for, and that gratitude, that wondering over His love, will cover us all. And it will carry us—carry us in ways we cannot comprehend.

—Kara Tippetts

I STILL REMEMBER THE ALBUM COVER. Yellow the color of a caution light. Black-and-white photo of the musician in a T-shirt, arms crossed, just enough of his face showing to reveal a smile, the name "Rich Mullins" in block letters. 1986. He was at the very beginning of his journey to reluctantly becoming one of Christian music's most famous stars. I was nine when I pulled the tape from the music display at my grandparents' bookstore.

I took the cassette home and played it over and over. I never knew it didn't sell very well. Or that Rich's next one didn't either. I didn't know about his wrestling match with loneliness and alcohol. I just closed my eyes and sang "Awesome God" along with the rest of my youth group. His first big hit, just in time.

I found out the backstory as I watched the movie *Ragamuffin* last night. I watched open-mouthed from my couch and cried so hard I had to get a roll of toilet paper from the bathroom as a substitute for tissues (that's how high-class we are in our house). At one point in the movie Rich listens to a recording of a message by author, speaker, and fellow struggler Brennan Manning about the unconditional love of God. Rich pulls off the road, gets out of the car, and drops to his knees, weeping in the grass and overwhelmed by grace.

I understand this completely. Because even as someone raised in church, someone who has written a book titled *You're Loved No Matter What*, and someone who has all the knowledge required to understand this fundamental truth, the grace of God sometimes still remains a vast mystery to me.

In my younger years, I stared at the names of authors in the aisles of bookstores, heard the words of speakers I respected, and listened to musicians belting out praise songs complete with electric keyboards and thought all these people must be perfect. I thought the same of many of the professionally religious adults in my life. I don't remember even sensing their struggles—perhaps I was just naive. Only later, as a grown-up myself, did I begin to find out about the divisions and affairs and addictions they warred against behind closed doors.

It seemed the prevailing mantra in those days was, "Be a good witness for Jesus." A positive example must be a flawless one. Fake it until you make it. But in so many ways, this led only to striving or rebellion. I watched as many of my peers drifted from the fold. Those who remained often leaned toward being performers and pleasers, the gold-star junkies. I counted myself among the latter.

The other night as I prayed, it seemed God whispered to my heart, "You think whatever you're trying to get control of is the real issue. But it's not—what's really the most destructive is the shame and guilt you allow in because of it."

This is why I cried when I watched the movie about Rich Mullins. And again as I read Brennan Manning's memoir, *All Is Grace*, just before I went to sleep. Because for so many years I didn't know—I really didn't—that someone could be used by God, especially in a very public way, and still be fighting battles every day. I feared human imperfections were actually divine disqualifications, and I was living on borrowed time when it came to God's willingness to work through me.

I didn't realize the authors I idolized on the shelves of my grand-parents' bookstore could have put a well-placed comma on the page and then, in a moment of weakness, snapped at their kids for interrupting them. Or the performer might have wrapped up their show then had too many beers alone in a hotel room, an un-fortunate self-prescription to dull the anxiety and exhaustion. The artist who created the beautiful piece about forgiveness perhaps did so only a few minutes after getting rid of the pornography.

I suppose I should have suspected this because of what I read in Scripture. After all, the man after God's own heart opened the door to adultery and murder. The wild-faith ark builder got drunk. The boldest disciple lied and denied in the most crucial moment.

Instead, it took a very long time for me to understand we are all broken. No level of spirituality or ministry exists where we are suddenly exempt from being human. I grieve for my own heart because of this. And for the thousands of other silent pew sitters and hopers throughout history who have thought the same. Who have nearly drowned in their shame. Who have told themselves, "I'm sure I'm the only one." And all the while Jesus has been waiting, hand extended, and simply saying, "This is why I came."

As I've talked about before, I'm still learning grace is not just for getting us into heaven—it is for getting us through this life. It is for the first sin and the millionth. It is for all we hide in the dark.

It is for the broken places that are like scabs knocked off over and over. It is for the thing we think excludes us.

I wish there had been less telling and more showing way back then when I first started looking for grace. I would have liked to see the scars from skirmishes fought with bare, tender hands. I would have liked to touch skinned knees from the falls. I would have liked to walk beside folks when they were still limping. I hope that is how I'm living, how I'm writing—*Jesus, may it be*.

The road may be straight and narrow but we are not. We are the stragglers and drunkards weaving side to side. We are the stumblers and strayers. We are the delayed and stubborn. We are the inexplicably cherished.

In *Ragamuffin*, Brennan Manning says, "I am now utterly convinced that on judgment day the Lord Jesus will ask one question and only one question, 'Did you believe that I loved you?'"[1] If this is so, I want to say yes loud and deep and clear, like a single note of music, like the start of a song that's meant to go on forever.

LET'S NEVER THINK
we are more *holy* or whole
than someone else.
WE MAY HAVE CRACKS
in different places,
BUT WE ARE **ALL**
still **broken** . . .
and still *beloved.*

kind,
Not Nice

The harder, braver choice? Kindness.
It's one of the most underrated virtues of our time.

—Jennifer Dukes Lee

SHE ARRIVES AMID CHATTER about swimsuit shopping (ugh!) and the anticipation of summer travel and which appetizer is calling our names. I know that look in her eyes—the one that says she is trying very hard to be brave. Someone asks how she is and she answers, "I'm not okay, but I will be."

We have questions and when we hear how she's been treated, we get defensive. There is talk of smacks and baseball bats and where to hide bodies. We are all bark and no bite, of course, but this is how we get when someone goes after one of our own. We are modern mama bears, and anyone in danger is the designated cub. Do not underestimate us.

My friend smiles for the first time that night and laughs at our antics, our silliness, our attempts to say, "We're sorry you're going through this, and we care a lot about you." Then we ask her what she's going to do. She says in all seriousness that she is going to be kind.

The next day another friend in a faraway place asks if we can talk on the phone. Our friendship is usually one of written words, so I know something must be different, must be urgent. I tell her yes, of course we can, and soon I'm listening to the sound of tears in her voice. I grip my phone as if doing so might somehow impart strength to her. She too has heard unexpected words that sting.

After we process what's happened, she asks, "Is this who I am? Am I really the person they described?" I tell her no, not at all, in a way that feels like a roar rising up inside me. I remind her of how she is beautiful, encouraging, and a gift. I want to hurl a china plate at the wall or stomp something to bits beneath my feet. I want to exile these people who hurt her to a remote island with only one palm tree. When I ask her what she's going to do, she says, just like my other friend, "I'm going to be kind."

If these friends of mine had said this to me a few years ago, I might have thought their answers were the same as "I'm going to be nice." But I know them, and I realize this is not what they mean. I have come to personally understand the difference between those two words as well—*nice* and *kind*.

My shift in perspective began a few months ago when an email shot into my inbox like a tiny arrow making its way straight to my heart. I drew in a sharp breath and pulled back from the keyboard. I knew the sender probably hadn't intended for her words to pierce—but they had. *Now what?*

In the past I would have pretended to be fine. I would have been tempted to sooth the wound with resentment and plaster on a smile the next time I interacted with her. In other words, I would have tried to be *nice*.

But recently God has been showing me that we aren't called to be nice. I searched Scripture and the word *nice* appears only four times—and every single instance is in regard to things, not people. I wondered about that until I realized that's what happens when we choose to be nice. We deny the parts of ourselves that make us human, like our emotions, wills, and hearts.

In contrast, the word *kind* appears more than 250 times in Scripture. We're specifically told, "Be kind to each other" (Eph. 4:32 NLT). So what is the difference between being nice and being kind? It essentially comes down to this: Nice comes from fear. Kindness comes from love.

Jesus was kind, but he was not nice. He spoke the truth from his heart. He dared to disappoint people. He obeyed God instead of trying to make everyone happy. Because of that he could truly love. Even on the cross, Jesus wasn't passively letting anyone take advantage of him. The crucifixion was part of a grander plan, a choice he made for his Father, for us, and "for the joy set before him" (Heb. 12:2). Let's never use his example to justify others treating us in ways God does not and will not ever condone.

We belong to a one-another God. His design includes mutual love, respect, and service. Extraordinary giving when God asks us to do so differs from continually ignoring or annihilating our own needs. As Harriet Braiker says in *The Disease to Please*, "You may choose to be a martyr and sacrifice your own needs on the altar of those of your family and friends. But, in doing so, you are neither demonstrating nor proving that you are unselfish, but merely self-destructive."[1]

Niceness comes from fear.

Kindness comes from love.

Niceness says, "I want to please you."

Kindness says, "I want the highest good for both of us."

Niceness says, "I will tell you what you want to hear."

Kindness says, "I will speak the truth with grace."

Niceness says, "It's okay if you habitually hurt me."

Kindness says, "It's not okay because hurting me hurts God, you, and us."

When we ignore the pain, when we give in to the fear, when we say yes when we mean no, over time our hearts form calluses out of self-protection. We can no longer be as hurt, but we can no longer care with the same tenderness either.

I put my fingers on the keyboard and type a reply to the hurtful email. Then I delete it. I try again and finally find the words—kind ones—to prevent this particular kind of arrow from flying my way. As I hit send, all the resentment disappears. I feel my heart open to this person again. I have protected what's between us. This time it's simple. But it's not always. Sometimes it takes weeks or months or years, blood and sweat and wells of tears.

I ask my two friends for an update a few days after our conversations. One has actually stood in front of the group of people who hurt her and spoken God-breathed words of boldness and beauty. She has chosen not to let herself be swayed or silenced. She will not walk away. She will stay. She will serve. When I hear this, I want to stand up and cheer.

My other friend has responded with great grace and patience beyond what I imagine myself to possess. She has shared some much-needed truth and remained steadfast to what is necessary to protect her heart. But she has decided to continue loving long on a winding, bumpy road. This, to me, is true resilience.

I will be the first to raise my hand and say it's hard as nails to live like this, and I often falter in it. But after years of experience, I can say this with certainty—*it's even harder not to*. So let's keep helping each other find the courage to be more than simply nice and instead be truly kind. This is not the choice of wimps; it is the choice of warriors. Having a soft heart in a hard world is courage, not weakness. We're stronger than we know, braver than we think, and the universe needs true, audacious kindness more than ever.

As R. J. Palacio says in the children's novel *Wonder*, "If every single person in this room made it a rule that wherever you are, whenever you can, you will try to act a little kinder than is necessary—the world really would be a better place. And if you do this, if you act just a little kinder than is necessary, someone else, somewhere, someday, may recognize in you, in every single one of you, the face of God."[2]

Oh, the *audacity*

> We have to be braver than we think we can be, because God is constantly calling us to be more than we are.
>
> —Madeleine L'Engle

THE HEAT HERDS KIDS toward the neighborhood pool like cattle in neon green shorts and purple swimsuits. We stay until our fingertips have deep-creased watermarks and we wear the smell of chlorine like cheap perfume. We play tag and chicken and toss quarters into corners so we can retrieve them again and again. Occasionally, we venture into the deep end and dare each other to leap off the diving board with hoots and splashes.

As we swim one day, my friend notices something suspicious in the deep end of the pool. A group of preschoolers has just departed under the close supervision of daycare workers, but the watchful eyes have clearly missed the "present" one child left behind (try not to think about it). The water contains enough chemicals to sanitize the entire Mediterranean Sea, but still, something has to be done.

My friend announces we will tell the lifeguards immediately. We climb out of the pool and dutifully march toward the stand where whistle-wearing teenagers look at us with disdain. "There's something that needs to be cleaned out of the deep end," my friend says with a clear finger point for emphasis. The lifeguards look at us, then at each other, and do the classic "so what?" shrug before turning back to their conversation about girls or muscles or girls with muscles.

Now we are indignant. Our recreational area has been defiled, and this shall not be overlooked or ignored. "Come on," my friend says with a tug on my arm. As we stride purposefully and righteously out to the bike rack, a plan begins to take shape. "Here's what we're going to do," my friend declares. "We're going to go home and change into our best clothes. Then we're going to ride to the country club and talk to the president." I agree this sounds like quite a brilliant scheme, so we hop on our bikes, head our separate ways, and promise to reconvene at a chosen spot once our wardrobe switches are complete.

My friend chooses a suit, complete with a tie and jacket. I wear a Laura Ashley dress with flowers and shoulder pads. We feel like agents of enforcement as we pedal with all our might down cracked sidewalks and across bumpy roads as curious neighbors look up from watering the grass or polishing their cars.

We arrive, breathless, at the front door of the country club. Now this is a fancy place. My parents aren't members, and I've only set foot in it a time or two. It has a dining room where folks stop by for Sunday brunch or to replenish their strength after a grueling round of golf. The club has rules about what to wear and how to act and who can enter. I feel quite intimidated, but my friend simply pushes open the front door like he owns the place.

A startled secretary appraises us, then asks with trained politeness what she can do for us. I hold my breath for a moment and wonder if we'll soon be strong-armed out the door by security or possibly carted off to jail. My friend proceeds to boldly announce, "We are here to see the president." The secretary's curiosity about a pair of sweaty, dressed-up nine-year-olds must have gotten the best of her, because instead of shooing us out the door, she simply replies, "Please wait here a moment." She steps inside a door, and we hear murmured bits of a conversation. Then she reappears with a smile on her face and says, "Right this way."

The president of the country club sits behind a sturdy oak desk in front of bookshelves. He wears a starched white shirt and has gel in his hair. I imagine if I lean in, he might smell like cigars. He peers at us with a not-unfriendly face and inquires quite professionally about the nature of our visit. "We have a complaint," my friend offers, which causes the president to raise his eyebrows. So we share the story of the unfortunate incident at the pool. The president says "hmm" and "uh-huh" and "I see." Then he thanks us for coming, shakes our hands, and escorts us back to the front door. He may have offered us each a piece of candy for our troubles. Once outside, we congratulate each other on our audacity with high fives.

I laugh when I think about that day because there were a thousand "nevers" we could have said, but we ignored them all.

"They'll never listen to us because we're just kids."

"They'll never let us into the country club."

"If they let us into the country club, they'll never let us talk to the president."

"If they let us talk to the president, he'll never take us seriously."

"If he takes us seriously, he'll never follow through because he's too busy."

Instead, we simply said, "We see something that isn't okay, so we're going to do what we can." I think sometimes as grown-ups we forget this approach is an option. We spend a lot of time philosophizing, debating, and analyzing. Or worrying, wringing our hands, and waiting. We forget that results aren't our responsibility.

Our part is putting on our best clothes and riding our bikes to the country club. It's wrapping an arm around the shoulders of a hurting friend. It's choosing kindness and love in a world filled with division and criticism. It's speaking up bravely in the meeting about the discrepancies on the spreadsheets. It's refusing to give any room to the "nevers" and instead remembering we serve a God of the "whatevers."

"Whatever situation we're in, God can use us to make a difference."

"Whatever we face, God is bigger."

"Whatever happens, God is with us and for us."

"Whatever obstacles we encounter, we can overcome them."

"Whatever this world may do, we're going to keep being courageous."

Like any wise person in office, the president of the country club made no immediate or impulsive promises that day. But from that day forward, we noticed that sometimes a grown-up would stop by the pool in an official-looking uniform. This person would survey the scene, occasionally rebuke the lifeguards, and then drive away. Each time this happened, my friend and I would look at each other with triumph in our eyes as if to say, "Oh yeah, we totally made that happen."

I'm not sure that was actually the case.

But it sure could have been.

It's always worth a try.

Involved

> Remember, you don't have to be mighty in stature to be mighty in battle. You don't have to be beautiful or strong, or even physically fit to change the world, you just have to know that far greater is he that is in you than he that is in the world.
>
> —Susie Larson

THE TEARS ARE LIKE SWIMMERS at the edge of a cliff this morning. They may dive at any second—unstoppable—and I will not be able to call them back. They'll break the clear blue surface of my day. I grab hold of the straps of their swimsuits, stretchy like rubber bands in my hands. "Don't," I whisper to them.

I think then of another time I grabbed hold of someone trying to escape. It was in the early evening dark in the parking lot outside my church. A thief had stolen something precious from someone I loved—snatched it right out of their grip—and I was determined to get it back. I could feel the adrenaline rushing through my veins like a raft on the Amazon River, the anger burning hot in my chest like a native bonfire on the shore. Somewhere inside me a little voice said, "This may not be the best idea," but I was beyond caring, past fearing the consequences.

I reached out and grabbed the flimsy T-shirt of this criminal and yanked hard. A startled ten-year-old face belonging to a boy my own age turned toward me, all freckles and red hair in the spotlight shining down from a corner of the building. "Give back my little brother's ball," I said in a tone as clear as an old-time sheriff's warning shot. He complied with a slightly amused look on his face. "Sorry," he said, his hands in the air as if I were about to cuff him, a classic mug-shot smirk on his face. Then he ran off into the night, undoubtedly to find other trouble.

I handed the basketball to my brother and only then did I realize something felt odd, just a little off.

I held my arm up to the light and noticed with alarm that the fourth finger on my right hand was bent suspiciously. Apparently my finger had become entangled in the transgressor's T-shirt. When I yanked hard to force him to turn around and face me, there were unintended consequences. Although it didn't hurt much, clearly something was wrong and I shrieked at a volume preteen girls normally reserve for boy-band concerts. A responsible adult came running. I showed her the predicament. "Oh my," she said with Southern sweetness, and then for emphasis, "Oh, my, my." I knew since I'd gotten the double "my" in that expression I was probably heading to the emergency room. Mothers of this region have a certain code. One "my" means pull out the Band-Aids, two means get a doctor involved, and three means you're probably heading on home to glory.

She called my mama, who had dropped us off for basketball practice with our friends while she tended to something else (it must have been very important because she almost always stayed with us). Then I was escorted to the front seat of a large van and hauled to the nearest medical facility, where my parents met me and the attending physician said, "Fracture." I had two options: surgery and a metal pin—I immediately made a face like a crazed jackal at this suggestion—or let it heal naturally and live with it a tad out of line. I was a kid. Scars were cool. I wanted to go home and eat three fudgesicles. I picked the latter and left with a silver splint, which I frequently lost or forgot to wear.

To this day when I look at that finger, I can see that it bends slightly at the end. It's not all that noticeable, just a tiny slant to the left, and most of the time I completely forget about it. But right now it's on my mind because the reason for this morning's tears reminds me of that scene in the parking lot long ago.

Something has been stolen from someone I love all over again. This is far more significant than a ball—it's a heart theft, a snatching of treasures like trust and friendship and respect and kindness. I only recently became aware of it, and I've been part of the process of trying to recover what's been lost. Just this morning I did the equivalent of reaching out and grabbing hold of the taker's shirt and it worked. But just like back then, a part of me feels a bit bent and broken inside now too.

It's easier not to get entangled in this life. It's simpler to let the bandit run off into midnight obscurity. It's safer to turn our heads and look the other way. But I don't think this is what we are called to by a Savior who left heaven to defeat "the thief" who "comes only to steal and kill and destroy" the things of our souls (John 10:10).

I think we, as women, all have moments when it's time to put on the superhero cape and come to the rescue. And when we do, because we are human, we will almost always wind up with the scars to prove it. These are our badges of honor. These are the bits of us that say, "I'm for you, and I'm willing to show it."

These scars belong to the mama standing up for the child who's being bullied. To the coworker who asks the outcast out to lunch. To the wife who fights on her knees for her marriage. To the teenager who walks away from the gossip. To you in any moment when you say, "The enemy is not getting away with it this time." And when I say "enemy," I'm not talking about each other or even about the person doing the stealing. I'm talking about the darkness itself.

Part of daring to be who we are, of living fiercehearted, is knowing when it's time to roar, when it's the moment to grab the shirt and yank hard, when it's worth the fractured finger or broken heart. In other words, when it's time to get *involved*. This is not always the choice we are to make. Some battles are not ours to fight. And knowing the difference takes a lot of wisdom and prayer and unnecessary bruises when we go running in anyway. But we learn. We become sneaky ninjas in tennis shoes and fuzzy slippers. We who are all softness and grace on the outside are tough as steel on the inside.

I think I'll let the divers leap from the cliff this morning if that's what they need to do. These tears are not signs of weakness. They are proof my heart is wild and alive and mighty. I clench my fists and feel my fourth finger leaning in to touch my third as if tapping an old friend on the shoulder to tell a secret. "You are still brave," it seems to say to me. "Yes, you are stronger than you feel today."

Let's get our **hands** dirty
and our *hearts* broken
and **rips** in the knees
of our favorite
pair of jeans.
Loving
LIKE JESUS
is not always **SAFE**
(but it's always worth it).

Not the
only one

We all are on a journey that will take us through loss and trials and difficulties. People are fighting things we know nothing about. Everyone struggles in some way. We don't know what God has asked anyone else to walk through.

—Jennifer Ueckert

I NOTICE THE MINIATURE CUPCAKES FIRST, of course. Lovely frosted little towers of chocolate and vanilla set on clear plastic plates with a simple, swirly design around the edges. I walk past one and see it has toppled over, messy and unsteady next to its stand-up sisters. I wink reassuringly at it. I have been there too.

I might yet be again tonight, I think as I look at a microphone perched on a stage. In a few minutes, I will stand behind it. I think of all the other times I've gone to speaking engagements and ended up doing something disastrous or at least embarrassing.

One time I finished speaking and went to the bathroom to freshen up. When I walked in, I thought, *That's a funny-looking sink*, but I carried on with reapplying my lip gloss and even had a sweet little moment of prayer. When I opened the door to leave, I came face-to-face with a startled man. I looked at him in equal surprise, swiveled my head toward the sign that did indeed say "M-E-N," then turned back and politely but forcefully declared, "Do not tell anyone!"

That very same conference had a beautiful spread of refreshments that I retreated to in order to regain my composure. I thought a few sips of water would do the trick. I reached for the little knob on the spout of a gorgeous glass water jar to fill my cup. In my rattled state, I twisted it too far—so far it came completely off. And then water began gushing out like Niagara Falls. I didn't have a clue how to stop it, so I just stood there in a panic, putting cup after cup underneath the spout until the deluge ceased. I imagined conference attendees standing in the water line and whispering, "Isn't that our workshop teacher? She must be really thirsty." Then I had to confess to the director that as an honored guest I had vandalized conference property.

But the awkwardness doesn't stop there. At another event, this one even more well attended and where I was a keynote speaker, I slipped backstage to have my microphone fitted. It had been a long, busy day, and I desperately needed a quick escape to the ladies' room. I asked if I had time and the sound team gave me the thumbs-up. As I slipped out the back door, I heard an eerie click behind me. I turned around, and sure enough, I had locked myself out of the banquet hall where I would soon be speaking. I was in the belly of a fancy hotel with no idea how to get back into that room. Fortunately, two employees walked by at about that time. They didn't speak much English but managed to interpret my crazed gesturing enough to first smile with amusement and then point me to a side door. Disaster narrowly averted.

So perhaps in addition to my introvert tendencies, I have a bit of speaker PTSD. Regardless, I decided this current occasion was worth the risk. So I came out of my speaking sabbatical for an (in)courage meet-up. I cofounded (in)courage years ago while still an employee at DaySpring. It's a website we first described as, "A bit like God's beach house. A place where you can put your sandy, dirty feet on the coffee table, laugh late into the night with friends, and perhaps hear God's voice clearer than anywhere else." When God asked me to transition out of DaySpring, he provided new folks to manage (in)courage. They have nurtured and grown it well. I still write for the site, though, and the leadership team kindly asked me to be one of the emcees for the evening.

When I first got the request, I replied, "This scares me silly!" But as I thought and prayed about it, I knew it was something I was to do. And the meet-up was casual, just an invitation to women in a particular city to come together for an evening of conversation and connection. And, yes, of course dessert. Even so, at the last minute I still considered giving in to my fear. Letting someone else do it. Handing the microphone right over.

But then I remembered one little phrase: *you're not the only one.* You see, I had been telling myself that the other women at the event would have it all together. Their hair would be freshly highlighted, lip gloss perfectly applied, and their lives (as well as kitchen cabinets) would be in proper order. They would show up overflowing with good cheer and never once think about hiding behind the cupcake tower. *Unlike me.*

Thankfully, Jesus had been showing me that we are all more alike than different. We are all broken. We are all beautiful. We are all in need of grace. We are all glory reflectors. We are the paradox people. So I accepted the invitation to speak and now the big moment has arrived. I step away from the cupcake table and up to the microphone so I can share my heart with the women who have been brave enough to show up too. I say something like this to the crowd:

> We've come here tonight to find ourselves among friends, as (in)courage says. And C. S. Lewis once wrote, "Friendship is the moment when one man says to another, 'What! You too? I

thought that no one but myself. . . .'"[1] If that's true, then the starting place for this evening is to stop believing the lie that we're the only one.

Look around this room.

You're not the only one who has struggled with an addiction.

You're not the only one whose heart has been shattered by a divorce.

You're not the only one who is worried no one will like you.

You're not the only one who wonders if God is still listening.

You're not the only one who desperately needs a night away from dirty laundry and loud children.

You're not the only one who has walked into the wrong restroom or broken the valuables or locked herself right out of where she really wanted to be.

This is what community means—it's saying even if the specifics of our lives and stories are different, we both understand what it means to be human and we choose to do that with each other rather than apart.

I also share that I've begun saying "You're not the only one" in another way too. I have said it to myself with capital letters, "You're not the *Only One*." In other words, "You're not Jesus." Last time I checked no one else on the planet is either.

This is excellent news because it means we don't have to save the world. We don't have to be perfect. We don't have to take care of everything and everyone all the time. There is only One who can do those things, and he's quite good at them. It also means there is Only One who is truly deserving of our glory and our honor and our praise. Our lives are not about us. They are about him. Yes and amen.

I eventually step off the stage to hug necks and, of course, find the coffee and cupcakes again. The frosting alone is worth not letting the lies and fears win. I also manage not to cause any sort of crisis for myself or others. And, really, that poor water jug is my only official and serious casualty in my extensive list of mishaps. I'd say that means maybe I've done fairly well after all. I imagine you have too—better than you probably know or feel.

So just in case we're facing something hard or scary in our lives today, I'll whisper the truth one more time: *you're not the only one.* And the only One who can do the impossible is always with us. We've got each other too, the whole unseen sisterhood stretched out through history—an imperfect and unstoppable force.

Hey There,
friend

Sisterhood will be scary, but it is worth it.

—Ellen Graf-Martin

I SECRETLY ALWAYS WANTED one of those friendship necklaces—the kind shaped like a heart and split right down the middle. You remember those, don't you? Each person in the friendship gets a half, and then you both wear them to tell the doubting world, "Someone likes me." Those necklaces always felt like a bit of tiny armor to me. Like owning one would help me deflect feelings of insecurity or being left out. It would be proof I was valuable goods as a friend. Maybe it would give the cool girl in junior high staring at the no-name-brand on my jeans somewhere else to look.

But as a grown-up I've come to see those little necklaces aren't really a great representation of what friendship is actually like. They're hard, stiff, and small. They can't bend, yield, or grow. Maybe that's part of the appeal—because for a long time I also wanted a friendship that was absolutely secure. No changes. No conflict. No misunderstandings. The problem with this expectation is that it ruled out all humans, including myself.

I looked at a scrapbook of my growing-up years recently. As I stared at faces belonging to those who were once the dearest folks in the world to me, I thought of how time has scattered us like dandelions, each to our different places on this spinning planet. I used to feel guilty about this because I am a person who likes to hold on to my people. I write your name on my heart and there is no eraser. And in a way that's true—I could message or call any of those old friends and it would be like picking up where we left off, like we hadn't missed a single beat. But I also know our relationships wouldn't be the same. Because, really, *we* are not the same.

And I'm coming to see this is right. Because friendship is really all about helping each other become who God intends for us to be tomorrow. My wild-hearted friends from the season of the swing and the Dream Machine brought out the brave in me. And I would need that braveness for the coming jungle of junior high. I also needed the girls who sat cross-legged on the flowered comforter of my bed in high school and talked for hours, the ones who taught me to be a listener and an encourager. I needed the grown-up friends who gave me the courage to start a blog and write books. The ones who convinced me over lattes that I really might have something to offer to the world.

Sometimes we get to have a friendship that stays the same for a very long time. But I believe this is the exception. Because there are moves and graduations and job changes and *life*—just plain old life. The human heart also simply has a limited capacity to deeply connect with more than a handful of people in any given time period. Research has shown our brains have the ability to have about five people we are truly close to and only about one hundred and fifty who we can even keep up with in the Christmas card kind of way.[1] When I learned this, I felt enormously relieved. Because in our social media world, it seems as though we should be capable of having endless friends. We're like the kids at the buffet who stare with wide eyes but end up holding our bellies and aching because we have tried to have it all.

What I think we can do is ask, "God, please purposefully put the friends in my life who you want me to have in this season." Then when we find those folks, we treat them well and forgive them (and ourselves) over and over. We love them like they are our own velveteen rabbits; we do not replace them with fancier, shinier versions who don't seem to have the lumps or bumps or odd habits. And we pray very hard that they will do the same for us.

Then, if God asks us to, we let them go one day—let them pack the moving van or take the dream job or jump into the deep end of raising kids where there is not much time for coffee dates. This is the part I do not like. But the miracle of grown-up friendship is that often what looks like an end is only a corner. And eventually we make our way back to each other again. That gives me hope.

A friend far away sent me flowers yesterday. They're sitting on my kitchen table. Some of the blooms are full and smiling. Others are still closed buds of green. I sent a thank-you note via email this morning and got back this reply: "The flowers will get even more beautiful as they open up."

Yes, I thought, *this is what friendship does in and for us*. Each friend opens up a new part of who we are. This process is slow. It can also stretch us to the point where we think we will break. But there is so much beauty in it too. We come from a garden, and the God who walked there said it isn't good for us to do life alone. Along with many other things, I think this is because we only really *become* with the help of other people.

I just heard a familiar Southern holler from across the coffee shop. A college friend I haven't seen in years rushed over to give me a hug. We talked a bit about old times and what life looks like for us now. I could see the girl she was way back then and the wife, mama, and woman she is today. I felt glad that I got to be part of her unfurling, that we got to share a few breaths of this sweet, brief life.

As I sat back down, I imagined what loveliness she'll bring forth tomorrow. When the smile lines are around her mouth and eyes, evidences of joy. When her children are grown and maybe her grandkids too. When she wraps a lifetime of memories around her like a coat of many colors in all the shades of wildflowers.

Later as I watch the door close behind her, separating us for now, I send her on her way with this unspoken, familiar wish. I hope I get at least a glimpse of you in full and riotous bloom, my friend.

farther, Not Faster

I TEXT A FRIEND: "Do you want to have dinner at our favorite place?" She replies, "Um, YES." Enough said. We take a seat in a cozy back booth and the waiter drops off salty chips and chunky salsa. As the bowl gets emptier, we start to go deeper. Past the catching up on kids and movies we've seen and the people we both know.

She's a writer too, and her words are getting ready to spread their wings even wider in this world. If you were sitting on the other side of the salsa, you might tell me how a new dream, like a patient egg, is hatching in your otherwise empty nest. Whisper of the side business you started that is unexpectedly growing like

171

a lovely, welcome weed. Rub your belly and talk of the little one to come. Speak of being part of a new ministry or company or group at school that makes you feel more alive. Declare you're ready to live in a more fiercehearted way. You sense change; you feel it rising like goose bumps along your arms and burning like a hot flame inside you.

It's in these moments that we carry wonder and fear like twins. And when this happens, we're tempted to back away from the ledge, to convince ourselves our wings aren't quite ready yet. Or, alternately, we try to make a Big Plan for whatever might be ahead. At least that's what I tend to do. I find articles. I search the internet. I make drawings on whiteboards. I create documents with bullet points. I might even throw in a PowerPoint presentation, just to be safe. And all this can be helpful. There is wisdom in preparation.

But there comes a point when what's empowering becomes discouraging. When we begin looking at others not for inspiration but to compare. When what we find no longer feels like tools that will help but stones that weigh us down. When that happens, it's time to pause and remember why we're doing this thing in the first place. And if we've made it this far, we usually know. After we remind ourselves of the why, we can ask, "What do I want this to look like in my life?"

If we don't ask this question, then we tend to focus on the folks we consider "successful" and think we need to be and act just like them. So-and-so launched their business by working eighty hours a week, so I need to also. This expert moved into a commune and never spoke to anyone again. The latest trendsetter insists network-ing with thousands of people is the only way to make the magic happen. On and on it goes.

When I decided to start running, I looked into training plans and types of shoes. I watched videos on form and pace. I'm fairly certain I was on the Ironman website more than once. And I might have read the biography of an Olympic athlete. But then this hap-pened: I actually went outside and started hitting the pavement. I quickly realized I would not be a marathon runner and speedster instantly and simultaneously. And I would not be an Ironwoman. Ever. For one thing, I run a bit like a domesticated duck—feet spread wide, all enthusiasm and no coordination. I don't mind this. I'm a cheetah on the inside. But it does have its limitations.

I still have to remind myself over and over of a basic principle I learned in my research and by experience. *Holley, today you can go farther or you can go faster. But you cannot do both.* When you're in training, that's usually the choice. And in life it is too. I know all the way to the bottom of my toes that I want to be a "farther" kind of person and writer.

I tell this to my friend sitting across the table from me. "We can do all the flashy things that people tell us are required," I say. "We can fill up our calendars until we're exhausted. We can be loud and out front all the time. But I'm convinced the people who live and work that way are sprinters. They'll move on and at the end of their lives they'll say, 'One time I wrote a book' or 'One time I did this cool thing.' And that will be enough. They're going for speed—not distance." This is not a criticism; sprinting has a time and place. I sprinted to get my master's degree. To finish my counseling internship. To launch a website. During a whirlwind season of speaking. But I have come to understand that while sprinting is doable, it is not sustainable.

So if you plan to do something not for a while but for as long as you can because you love it, feel called to it, and the touch of heaven is on it, then sprinting is not the solution. Instead, live and work like you're going the distance. This means intentionally choosing a different pace. It means showing up over and over. It means letting people pass you. It means refusing to give in to the fear that you should always be doing more and instead continuing to faithfully, unglamorously do what matters most.

For me professionally and personally, this means *I just want to love God and people well for a long time.* When I first said this out loud, tears came to my eyes. Because it felt like coming home.

It took me years of frustration and exhaustion to realize this, to understand I'm built more for slow and steady. Finally saying those words also felt like the moment when I'm running and everything has been awkward, painful, and harder than it should be, but then I take one more step and it all clicks into place. My breathing evens out, my feet go where they're supposed to, my arms swing with new energy. I find my rhythm—the way I was born to run—and it feels entirely new and familiar all at once.

"Let us run with endurance the race marked out for us" (Heb. 12:1 NLT). That one word—*endurance*—says to me that life is not all sprinting. Faith, as Eugene Peterson says, is about "a long obedience in the same direction."[1] This makes no sense in our instant world. It's upside down in the time of social media updates. It seems less sexy and exciting than the fast and the fancy. But it's reassuring too, isn't it? To know we don't have to push so hard. We don't have to go big or go home. We can just be obedient and leave the results to God.

I hope sometimes we get to go fast. That there are moments with the wind in our hair, the hearts in our chests pumping wildly, and the ground a blur beneath our feet. But I'm asking Jesus even more that we go far. That we make it around all the bends in the road. Watch the leaves turn from green to amber gold. Have like-hearted companions with us—the kind who will share chips and salsa with us on an ordinary Tuesday evening. Take the next step, then the next step, all the way.

Let's keep running our race at our pace. We're doing better than we know.

See you at the finish.

38

Everyday
faithful

I'M AN HONORARY MEMBER in a club of vibrant ladies mostly in their eighties. They voted me in during one especially raucous restaurant lunch. When I returned, unsuspecting, to the table from the restroom, they announced with wide grins, "You're officially one of us!" I had no idea this impromptu process was taking place while I washed my hands and reapplied lip gloss. But I felt grateful for it nonetheless and immediately accepted. Who wouldn't?

The reality is I don't qualify for this standing on my own merit. I'm certain that had I suddenly appeared and given a speech about why I should be included, I would have been told, "Wait a few decades, sweetie." But I have a secret weapon: my grandmother, Eula Armstrong. She's been the teacher of their class at church on

Sundays for ages and they adore her. She first began inviting me to visit their group when I moved close by for college and lived only about an hour away from her. From time to time I would drop in to listen quietly to these women who have loved Jesus for a lifetime and each another for just about as long. They've prayed for me, watched me get married, supported me as I've birthed many books, and now they have decided I belong to them forever.

Usually they meet at someone's home for their socials. When they're at my grandma's house, I do my best to make the hour drive and pop in to catch up. They serve steaming soup from crockpots, with slabs of golden brown cornbread. The desserts are potluck, and it's common to find fudge marble cake sitting right next to a neon red Jell-O salad topped with marshmallows beside a fruit pie too, of course. They eat and laugh and play games like "Name that Hymn," which involves someone playing a few notes on a keyboard as the others shout over each other trying to guess. Many of them are widows. Some of them have lost children. They have seen the barest skin of life and have still called it beautiful.

Their friendships are my favorite kind. The sort where they can say, "Remember that summer back in 1968 . . ." They've looked into each other's faces at all ages. Rocked each other's babies. Stood together at funerals. Waved hello and goodbye in the church parking lot sporting dozens of hairstyles and hemlines. It's a deep-rooted affection that is rare. And my grandma guards those bonds. A phone call or casserole when someone gets sick. Closed lips like a fire extinguisher pointed toward gossip or division. Handwritten cards for birthdays or losses or no reason at all.

My grandma grew up in dust, a child of the Depression era who lived in a little place called Potato Hill. She sometimes says with a half smile, "We were so poor the poor folks were ashamed of us." She married my grandpa at age fifteen and brought my father into this world barely a year after. My aunt followed a short time later. Not yet twenty, my grandma had two kids, a husband, and a job in a cookie factory.

Faith had been part of her family's life growing up, but it was not until her twenties that she fully took hold of how much God loved her and this changed everything. After dropping out of high school when she married, she eventually completed not only an undergraduate degree but a master's as well. She became a youth minister—the first woman to hold the position in her church—and was affectionately called "Brother Eula." She eventually took a role at the Arkansas Baptist Children's Home working with kids whose pasts were as rock-hard as her own beginnings. Most recently she taught eleventh- and twelfth-grade English in a high school, the two years she missed. When asked about all this, her eyes get misty and she says, "The Lord restores."

Many of my childhood memories are of the years when she worked for the children's home. She and my grandfather lived in an apartment on the top floor of a traditional redbrick building with white wooden trim at the end of a circular drive. When we visited the children's home, my brother and I swam in a pool where startled goldfish occasionally and mysteriously appeared. We jumped on a trampoline with squeaky springs in the gym and rode horses at the stable, including a chestnut-brown mare with a white stripe down her nose who I nicknamed Cocoa. We made friends with the kids who lived at the home, including a boy named Peanut, who developed a crush on me in third grade and asked if he could give me a ride on the handlebars of his bike. "My grandma wouldn't like that," I answered solemnly.

I remember one evening coming with my grandma to a meeting of all the youth at the home. We sang and watched a brief video. Someone shared a message. And there was my Eula in the middle of it all. Just like now. She's a people gatherer and still says every time I come to see her, "Open door, open heart." It's not just a figure of speech to her; it's the way she does her living.

And this is a reminder to me of something my soul needs to know. I have not yet seen her likeness on a billboard in Times Square. Her name is not emblazoned in lights or splashed across a magazine cover. Yet to this day her phone rings with calls that start, "We knew each other years ago and you may not remember me, but here's how you touched my life . . ." When I visit her class, it's much the same. Someone will slip an arm around my shoulder and tell me what my grandma did to help them. Most of the time no one else ever knows what she's done. She loves well with humility and stunning consistency. Living this way is nothing remarkable to her, but it is to me. And, I'm certain, it is to the Jesus she serves.

I think of those words we long to hear, the ones we've talked about before. "Well done, my good and faithful servant" (Matt. 25:21). There is no exclamation point. No extravagant adjectives. No long and complex explanation. There is simplicity. It sounds like not one BIG accomplishment but instead a lifetime of obedience. So ordinary you might miss it if you're not paying attention.

But I'm paying attention these days. I'm holding a bowl of soup in my grandmother's kitchen, and it's warm in my hands. I draw it closer to my face to smell the broth and peer over the rim at a room of women. They are lovely. I watch one put a hand on another's knee. I see one throw her head back with laughter. I notice the nods and what's said without words after years of practice. And my grandmother is in the center again, just about to clear her throat and announce it's time to say the blessing.

In a moment they'll bow their heads and speak to Someone they've loved for a long time. After the "Amen," they'll motion me over to a seat, and I will sit with them because, after all, I'm official now.

And I still have so much to learn.

What I
know now

MY BEAUTIFUL DAUGHTER will graduate college today.
She'll walk boldly across a stage in front of a crowd of folks who
either love her dearly or don't know her a bit. She'll wear a cap on
curled hair and a gown over a pretty yellow dress we picked out
together. I'll applaud and feel like all the clapping in the world
would not be enough to cover it.

And I will also think of a day not that long ago, or so it feels, that I
walked across a stage too. There are some things I wish someone had
told me then. I'm saying them now. Better late than never, I suppose.

Dear Younger Me,

*You are twenty-two and it feels like you know everything.
When you are thirty-eight, you will think you know nothing at all. What's actually true is probably somewhere in*

179

the middle. So let's just make a deal that we'll always keep learning.

You are fixated on the starting line of your career. But moving forward is not really about getting a job. You already have a job. It is to become all God created you to be. You've had it since you drew in your first breath and you'll have it until you release your last. Everything in between is just about assignments, different experiences that will help with the becoming.

Work of any kind can be a holy, sacred thing. It can be just as much worship as church singing on a Sunday morning. Sometimes maybe more. So don't let anyone trick you into believing what you're on earth to do can easily be printed on a business card or typed in neat lines on a resume. You are on this earth to be—which is really just another way of saying you're here to love and be loved.

If this world can't talk you into believing your job is your identity then it will choose convincing you to be busy as a backup. "How are you?" we all ask each other. "Busy," we answer with a sigh and a secret bit of pride. Because busy means we are wanted. Busy means we have been chosen. Busy means we are earning our keep.

Let me forewarn: I have lived busy. I have breathed it and fallen asleep to it and cried in the bathroom because of it. I know what it is to be stretched thin, so thin that anyone could see right through to the empty places I was trying to fill with a few more scribbles on my calendar. It is okay to have a lot to do, especially if it aligns with who you're created to be and what you're called to accomplish. This is not the same as being busy. There is one question that can help us tell the difference. I wish I had learned to use it long before now. It would have saved us a lot of pain and exhaustion. We can ask, "Am I doing this out of fear or out of love?" Busy is always afraid.

One reason you choose to be so busy is because you think you have to make up for what you lack. You think you don't have a right to just dwell on this planet like other people. You don't deserve to have freely offered affection. So you hustle for those things. Don't hustle—you don't have to. You are enough as you are, and those who find you lacking will not be satisfied no matter how you stretch yourself to meet their expectations. Better to know that right away and let them go looking elsewhere for a human pretzel.

Also, you don't have to turn yourself into an extrovert. Goodness knows you've tried. You just spent three years living in a house with eighty other girls. I know you survived by escaping to the library and bookstore. This will not change. But what you don't have to do is be ashamed of your quietness and thoughtfulness. Just like your louder sisters don't need to be ashamed of their exuberance or ability to speak their minds spontaneously. There's no use fighting who you are because it's not going to change much. You're only going to become more you. So lean into it. Pay attention to it. Your greatest strengths are in the places you think you're least likely to find them now.

A related side note: When it comes to who you choose to have in your life, pick quality over quantity. You are afraid of being left out or left behind. This means you will sometimes let people have access to your heart who do not appreciate it or treat it well. This is not necessary and you will not be alone if you stop it. Know your worth—and only choose to let people deeply know you if they see it too.

About faith, let's try not to be quite so set in the preference and opinion parts. Right now you think in black and white but God is color and mystery. Yes, hold on to the few non-negotiables. But keep the rest in open palms, especially the things that sometimes make you feel like you might be better than some others. You're not. We're all just clay on the wheel, which is another way of saying we are dust being sculpted into glory. This is not our doing. And the secret of clay is that it knows how to yield, how to continue being shaped. Stay close to the Maker; let the transforming come and do not be afraid of it. Also, do not be afraid of people who are being made into something other than you. It's a bare table that has only one bowl.

Worry is as hurtful a habit as drinking too much or smoking and is just as likely to kill you. And you, sweet girl, are a ten-packs-a-day worrier. I'll let you in on a little secret—almost none of the things you worry about are going to happen. And the very, very few that do are going to turn out to be the doors to some of God's most beautiful and healing work in your life.

This might be my only regret so far: I have let worry run off with my joy like a thief in the night over and over again. Lock the door and bar the windows of your heart to worry this second, honey. The real danger is not what you imagine might happen but the thief himself. You're really so much more secure than you feel.

At a certain point, you are going to get some attention. This is going to confuse you because your insides are allergic to it. At first you will deal with this by immersing yourself in it, by trying to do everything and serve everyone because you are terrified someone will think that you think you are more special than them. Then this will become exhausting and you will hide for a while. At last you will realize that it's not about you and not about them. Instead, this is all just an opportunity to bring attention to Someone Else. With time, conversations, and counseling you will be alright again. All this is okay. So be kind to yourself. You're doing the best you can.

Of all the folks who will come in and out of your life, you only get to keep two for the whole ride: yourself and

Jesus. So it makes good sense to learn to treat yourself with the same courtesy you show others. Right now you are a perfectionist. You would go straight to HR to demand better working conditions if an actual boss affronted you in such ways. But you can't recognize that in the mirror today. You only think this is how things must be. Someday you will understand more about grace. But even then it will be a long stretch before you truly embrace it for yourself. Might as well go ahead and add that to your little to-do list.

Finally, you are actually quite wonderful. This isn't something you can see yet or anything you even feel most days. Have the courage to start believing it anyway, because contrary to what you fear, it will humble you. It will make you lift your hands in praise to the One who made you. And then extend those same hands to bless those around you. This does not seem like it would be true, but in the upside-down kingdom, it is so.

I'm cheering for you.

XOXO,
Holley

LET'S REMEMBER
we are *all* still in
the **middle** of the
MESSY, BEAUTIFUL WORK
of *becoming*

casseroles,
Yodels, Love

Jesus, Your words give me courage to become
who You've created me to be.

—Renee Swope

IT'S A SMALL TOWN tucked into the middle of a state like a
rock in a child's pocket. It's rough and worn like the grizzled face
of an old man who has known hard times and survived them. Mark
and I pass the tattoo parlors, pawn shops, boarded-up windows,
and gas stations that sell fried chicken and chow mein. A chain-link
fence wraps around a warehouse. I'm delighted with the dachshund
guard dog stretched out like a happy sausage in the yard.

Eventually we pull into the parking lot of the funeral home. It's
smack in between the hospital and the cemetery. This seems both
thoughtful and efficient. On the other side is the third assembly
church. I briefly wonder how high the numbers go. Perhaps there
is a twelfth or a forty-second in this town of only a bit more than
a handful of folks.

We go inside, expecting to find it hushed like such places tend to be. But instead we're surrounded by chatter and laughter, hugs and it's-so-good-to-see-you's. It's a farewell and a family reunion and a celebration all in one. The guest of honor is at the front, and I don't think she'd mind this. She has slipped home to Jesus after a long, full life and a valiant battle with cancer. She liked to travel, this woman, deciding to spend her retirement years volunteering on various continents. We are here as the send-off party, the goodbye wavers you see in old movies as the grand ship pulls away.

After the greetings are done, I sit in a pew covered with something surprisingly like turquoise carpet and consider the affection and recollections I've heard secondhand. We didn't know this woman well but want to offer our comfort to those who did. This leads me to reflect, as these occasions tend to do, on all relationships. "What's on your mind?" Mark asks. He's known me long enough now to recognize when I'm contemplating. I say, "You might think it's crazy." He shrugs his shoulders, so I carry on. "I was thinking of different people in my life and how I would feel if this service was for one of them. Would I have regrets? Is there anything I want to start doing differently now so I'll be ready for then? What would I want to be able to say on that day?"

I think of this all through the evening and the service the next day too. I think of it as I go to sleep that night in a place far from home. I let memories play in my mind. I see the beautiful days, falling like snowflakes, and I catch them like a child in a red coat, open-mouthed with her face toward the sky. I recall the loving words and the laughter. They warm me. But like a kaleidoscope shifting, I can also recall the moments when feelings were hurt. The chill of words I wish could be unsaid. The times of anger and frustration and fear. We are human, and we struggle to love each other well even when we want to. Oh, how we want to. But we are clumsy with each other's hearts.

At first this bothers me. I wish for a time machine that could take me back, back, back for a second try. I would do certain events, particular conversations, differently if I knew then what I know now. But that is not how this life works. We write in cement and not in pencil. The past is set.

Faced with this reality, I decide, in the end, this is what matters: conflict is inevitable; kindness is optional. If we share life long enough with someone, anyone, then there will be misunderstandings and toes stepped on or circumstances that stretch us apart like snappy rubber bands. What matters is not if that happens but what we do when it does. Do we go searching for the perfect people with whom we will never experience such things, forgetting this is impossible because we ourselves are not such a person? Or do we forgive, even if it's sometimes slowly and from a heart-safe distance, believing the way back to each other can start with the smallest of steps.

These are the questions that will make the difference when we are sitting in a pew and there's a hymn about heaven and the scent of so many flowers in the air. Years ago I would have wanted to be able to say, "We had the perfect relationship." But this is like longing for Santa Claus or the tooth fairy to show up and do the eulogy. It's a lovely, impossible dream. There are always only ordinary mortals in the room, doing what we can, and letting a God who is divine love fill in the gaps for us.

After the service we go to the fellowship hall of a little church, a sweet country one with open doors and hearts. I am familiar with such events, and in the car on the way, I make predictions to my husband. "There will be a casserole with cream of mushroom. A salad with hard-boiled eggs. A berry cobbler." I am not disappointed.

The older ladies of the church, silver-haired and smiling, hold ladles and spoons and urge us to have seconds. So we feast on this day of sorrow. We eat our fill and wipe our mouths with white paper napkins. We have seconds of everything and tell stories about the one gone home. It's a blessed juxtaposition, this ritual. That on the day of loss there are always people to come around and place something nourishing into the emptiness, as if to remind us we will not feel so hollowed out forever.

At the end of the meal, one of the women, slender and dignified, stands up and yodels. I'm startled and amazed. Someone whispers to me, "She always does that." Then she tells a story of being a teenager on a church bus with this same woman on a youth trip and how she yodeled then too. I think this is wonderfully odd and endearing. A fitting benediction as we sit there around plates emptied of cornbread and green beans with bacon.

When the yodeler is done, it's time to go. So we wrap arms around necks and sneak one last pinch of cake when no one is looking. We say, "Nice to meet you" and "See you soon" and "She really was a remarkable woman." They are the sort of words we say on days like these, comforting in their familiarity and kindness.

All weekend I have wrestled with what I would want to be able to say when it's time for other goodbyes. When I release the hands of those I love into the hands of Jesus. Or when they do the same for me. Somehow in this little fellowship hall, with my feet on the threshold of the door, I think I finally know.

It's simply this: "We learned to live fully and love bravely." It's not a poem or a declaration. It's not a manifesto or a creed. Not a doctrine or a proclamation. It's just what I still believe deep down we all can do. It's the story of the fiercehearted.

And I know in that instant somehow it will be enough. Enough to let joy into the room so it can stand with its arm around the shoulder of grief. Enough to fill a casserole dish until there are delicious burnt bits running down the edges. Enough to sound like a great yodel sent out to the universe, a kind of ordinary, miraculous roar that echoes past a lifetime.

Epilogue

It's never too late for a happily ever after.
—Lovelle Gerth-Myers

I KNOW THIS WAITING ROOM. The beige textured walls and the home channel comfortingly playing on the television in the corner. The photos of babies, round cheeks like peaches, sleeping peacefully folded in blankets or the arms of siblings. This morning the room is full of lovely round-bellied women, each in different stages of pregnancy like the phases of the moon. This is the same waiting room where Mark and I came so many times, where I said prayers that sometimes felt like wishes on a star that one day we'd have a baby in our lives.

Our path back to this place began months ago, the day before my Mama's birthday. I remember where I was, sitting cross-legged on the rug in my brother's living room, wrestling with one of my nephews. My phone rang and Lovelle's name appeared on the screen. The air swirled with giggles and shrieks, so I put one finger in my ear when I answered. Emotion in her voice. I stretched my legs and rose, walked into a little-boy bedroom with a fish tank and a light like a disco ball. "What did you say?" I asked. She repeated, "I'm pregnant."

And I spun backward, sat right down on the small bed as if I was five again myself, the time when the world seems so big and nothing impossible. She asked, "Mom? Are you there? What do you think?"

The timing had come earlier than she and David planned, but somehow I'd known. For weeks. I knew it when we'd cut the leg off a roasted turkey on the Thanksgiving table. I'd known when we roared at a hockey game while the players below shoved each other into thick plastic walls. I'd known when she'd said she was tired and wanted her pajamas at four in the afternoon one day.

I'm thrilled.

"What? How did you know?" she's inquiring, and I can't fully explain. It's as if God has given me a divine heads-up to ready my heart. And right there in Texas, not far from where I grew up, with my sweet mama and daddy in the next room and my God-given child on the phone, my whole world tilts on its axis.

It hasn't righted itself since and I've been spinning, spinning, with the joy of dreams fulfilled and hopes granted and thoughts of onesies with tiny animals on the front. Not long ago marked twenty weeks in Lovelle's pregnancy. She asked, "Do you and Dad want to come with David and me to find out the gender?" I answered, yes, of course.

And now we're in this waiting room again in the middle of a story only God could write.

A nurse calls Lovelle's name. We go to a small room and the three of us—Mark, David, and I—stand against the wall as if we're there for a police lineup. Lovelle stretches out on a table and the nurse places an ultrasound wand against her skin. I hear the rush and whoosh, the sound of wind across a canyon, the depth of the oceans, the story seashells tell when you hold them up to your ear, something like a breath or maybe a kiss blown into air.

I hold my breath for a moment until the nurse says, "Everything is fine." The four of us watch the monitor and we see this baby, our family's baby, and it is wonder and miracle. The baby is moving, turning somersaults or swimming laps or whatever other activities occupy womb time. At one point it looks like the baby is running, little feet up and down, up and down. I laugh out loud and say to Lovelle, "This baby is going to be a lot like you." She grins, a new smile I haven't seen her wear before, the proud mama kind.

The nurse explains the black-and-white images to us. She points out the nose, lips, fingers, arms, legs, toes. She focuses on the heart for quite a while and we watch as it beats, beats, beats with new life. "One hundred forty-one beats a minute," she says. "That's strong."

Then the moment comes we've all been anticipating. "The gender is clear," she tells us. She speaks it out loud. We gasp and clap and Lovelle gets teary-eyed. I want to shout it, write it across the sky, open the door and share the news with whoever passes by.

But David and Lovelle have decided to do a gender reveal party for close family and friends. So for the next few days, the four of us and the hostess for the party will be the only ones who know this secret. I carry it around like a diamond in my pocket, turn it over and over again, guard it, and pull it out to look at it, amazed and grateful.

The day of the party comes and we gather at Lovelle's house. I help her mother-in-law hang pink and blue balloons—no early clues allowed. The hostess has brought giant crepe paper flowers in those colors too. There are tiny rubber ducks that will float in drinks and little grey elephants scattered around the house, Lovelle's theme choice for the nursery.

Guests arrive and we exchange the usual small talk. Folks record their votes—girl or boy—on a chalkboard. Every time I look, "boy" is in the lead. At three o'clock we're called to the dining room to face a wall dotted with more balloons. "A piece of paper with the gender of the baby is inside one," Lovelle says. "You have to pop them to find out." One at a time guests step up. Confetti bursts out from each balloon. Bits of color rain down on our clothes and the hardwood floor. Only one balloon remains. Someone figures it out, "The gender isn't in there. This is an April Fool's joke!" It's true—Lovelle couldn't resists taking advantage of the date on the calendar.

The hostess brings a cake from the kitchen, white icing and the words "Little girl or little boy?" scrolled across the top in pink and blue. Lovelle takes the knife, slices, pauses for effect, then tips the piece on its side to reveal the color. She stares in confusion. I squint. Mark leans in. David tilts his head. Because there, in the middle of the cake that's supposed to hold the answer, is only blankness. A carrot-cake color revealing nothing.

The hostess laughs and laughs. "April Fool's on *you!*" she exclaims to Lovelle. My daughter, delighted, joins in the merriment and rushes to hug her, declaring, "You got me good!"

Then the husband of the hostess sneaks into the room holding an Easter basket with a giant green egg in it, the plastic sort you pull open and hide treasures inside. The crowd begins to understand this will be the real deal, the big reveal. Lovelle gleefully grabs the egg and inside . . . pink! But then, that egg opens too and . . . blue! The tension builds. Another egg and . . . pink! One more to go.

In that moment it feels as if time suspends itself. Like I somehow hit "pause" on the scene in front of me and step back from it. I watch other scenes play in my mind. I am a girl in her twenties holding a pregnancy test. I am on a table in a doctor's office hearing hard news. I am birthing books. I am meeting Lovelle, tiara in her hair. I am watching her walk down the aisle. I am answering the phone and hearing her voice, "I'm pregnant."

The sorrow and the longing and the joy are light and dark threads. Lovelle's story, my story, woven together in ways only God could have fashioned. I think about the two of us and how we've known heartache and hope and everything in between. How we both know what it is to fall asleep with tears still on our cheeks, to dream, to wake up again to keep pressing in and pressing on when it would be easier to give up. To keep our hearts open when it seemed safer to shut them forever. To hold on to our belief that God is never, ever done with our stories.

I think of all my sisters, women like you, who are strong and courageous and brave too.

Then I think of this baby. The one already turning somersaults. I can't wait to have this little one in my arms—living, breathing redemption. I am a mother. I am becoming a grandmother. The story continues.

Lovelle opens the last egg. There are cheers. Happy tears. Clicks of cameras. It's only been days since I heard what everyone else is finding out now, but it feels like I've known so long, as if it has been weeks or years or all my life. "One hundred forty-one beats a minute," the nurse said. "That's strong."

This baby is a girl.

I pray one day she'll be a fiercehearted woman.

a *fierce* HEARTED WOMAN . . .

looks life in the face and says, "You can't beat me."

Knows *love* is risk but reaches out anyway.

Understands *kindness* takes real courage.

BELIEVES THE IMPOSSIBLE.

Fights like she's unstoppable.

Dares to find beauty in a ragged soul.

Scandalously picks warm over cool.

Tastes life as a brief, salty-sweet miracle.

Skins her knees, has scars that bear witness.

Defends like a warrior and weeps like a girl.

Makes gentle the new strong, small the new big,

ordinary the new extraordinary.

Sees wrinkles on a face as lines in a victory story.

NEVER GIVES IN, NEVER GIVES UP, NEVER LETS GO.

Chases Jesus with a tender, world-changing wildness.

Lives in your neighborhood or not even on your continent.

Looked back at you from the mirror this morning . . .

and has yet to fully see the force her star-scattering,

mountain-moving, water-walking *God created her* TO BE.

Discussion Questions

For you. And your fiercehearted people. Talk about it, y'all.

1. *Unexpectedly Fiercehearted*—What's a moment in your life when you became a little more fiercehearted?
2. *Being Woman*—What messages did you hear about being a woman as you were growing up? What do you believe is true now?
3. *Dream Machine*—What dream have you had that turned out differently than you planned? What did it teach you or how did it change you?
4. *Scratches on the Wall*—What part of who you are have you struggled to accept? What's one way your life would be different if you dared to do so?
5. *Hiding in Stalls*—Are you an introvert or an extrovert? How is that both a challenge and a strength for you?
6. *Swing Hard*—Have you ever had to defend someone or something you value? Describe what happened.
7. *Muddy Glory*—What do you think childlike faith really means? Include a story about a child in your life as an example if you can.

8. *Mango Closet*—Have you ever rebelled, even just a little? What brought you out of your rebellion and how did grace play a part in that change?

9. *Off the Shelf*—What story are you living right now? What helps you be fully present in it?

10. *Outside the (Pink) Lines*—Have you ever waited for something you really wanted? What gave you hope when you didn't know what would happen?

11. *Bone in the Chicken*—Can you think of a time when you wanted to impress someone, but it didn't go like you thought it would? What did you learn?

12. *Shake the Jar*—Do you ever struggle with doubt or have questions about what you believe? What helps you embrace the mystery of faith?

13. *Flops and Rafters*—Have you ever messed up even though you really intended to do better? What would you tell someone who just did the same?

14. *Praying Wronger*—What are your prayers usually like? When do you feel closest to God?

15. *Room for Knobs*—What's something you've held on to, now or in the past? What do you think is a secret to letting go and moving forward when it's time to do so?

16. *Wearing the Hat*—Do you have a "hat" in your closet like the writer one? If so, share a bit about it. If not (which is totally okay), share about a hat that someone you love has and how you encourage them.

17. *Shiny Rocks*—What do you think we're afraid of when we strive and try to prove our worth? What do our hearts really need to hear in those moments?

18. *Red Teapot*—What's a challenging relationship in your life (past or present)? What has it shown you about what you can and can't control?

19. *Like Water into Wine*—When have you unexpectedly felt wild joy or holy gladness? Share that story.

20. *The Ride*—Have you ever been in a place where you weren't sure what Jesus was doing or where he was taking you? What happened next?

21. *Crazy Sparks*—Do you like familiarity or novelty? How does your preference impact your everyday life and relationships?

22. *Ordinary, Divine*—What's a small moment in your life that somehow felt sacred to you?

23. *All Favorites*—Who tends to intimidate you? What's one thing that would help us look at each other differently?

24. *Cheeky*—What, if anything, has kept you from feeling fully beautiful? How might God see that part of you differently than you do?

25. *Get a Hanky*—Are you a reluctant crier or do tears come easily? When's the last time you cried and how did those tears help?

26. *Emotional Duct Tape*—What do you tend to do to "hold it all together"? What gives you the strength to let go and just know you're loved as you are?

27. *Pedicures, Mice, Therapy*—What have you heard about counseling? If you've gone, what has been helpful about it? What or who gives you courage when there's a "mouse" in your life?

28. *Brave, Hard Thing*—What brave, hard thing have you done for yourself in the past or need to do for yourself now?

29. *Different Kind of Sad*—What's a battle you've fought in your life? What would you say to someone facing a similar situation?

30. *Showing Up*—Why do you think we are sometimes afraid to be seen close up as we really are? Describe a time when someone saw you as you were and loved you that way.

31. *On Ragamuffins*—How have you seen someone you admire walk through a struggle and overcome it? What did you learn from their story?

32. *Kind, Not Nice*—How would you personally describe the difference between *kind* and *nice*? When have you witnessed or experienced true kindness?

33. *Oh, the Audacity*—Think of a time when you knew something needed to change and you took action, even if it was a little thing. What did you do?

34. *Involved*—When have you been brave on someone else's behalf, or when has someone else been brave for you?

35. *Not the Only One*—What's something in your life that tends to make you say, "I'm the only one who . . ."? What's actually true?

36. *Hey There, Friend*—How has God used a friend to help you become who you are today?

37. *Farther, Not Faster*—What next little step is God asking you to take in your life?

38. *Everyday Faithful*—Who in your life has lived and loved well for a long time? How have they done so?

39. *What I Know Now*—What would you say to your younger self?

40. *Casseroles, Yodels, Love*—What does being fiercehearted for a lifetime mean to you? Who do you want to share that journey with you?

Acknowledgments

Writing this book has reminded me again that life is a journey and those who walk with us make all the difference.

Thank you to my wonderful team at Revell—Jennifer Leep, Wendy Wetzel, Amy Ballor, and Brittany Miller. You are not only fantastic partners but also dear friends. I'm so grateful for the years we've spent together, and I look forward to what's ahead!

To my virtual assistant, Kaitlyn Bouchillon—Your diligence, excellence, creativity, and friendship matter more than you could ever know. I appreciate all you do.

To my parents, Don and Lyn Armstrong—I'm so thankful for all the wonderful memories I have because of you. You love me so well and pray for me so faithfully. So much of who I have become is because of you.

To my grandmother, Eula Armstrong—I am so blessed by the legacy of faith you have given me. You are an example of resilience and following Jesus for a lifetime. I'm so proud of you.

To my daughter, Lovelle—You are a gift from God to your Dad and me. We are grateful every day that he brought us together. You are a remarkable woman and were worth every minute of the wait.

To my husband, Mark—There are hardly enough words to describe all you are to me. Partner, friend, encourager, and the man I will be in love with all my life. I'm thankful every day to share this adventure with you.

To my dear friends who were cheerleaders, advisors, and prayer warriors while I wrote this book, especially Kim Sawatzky, Kristen Strong, Jennifer Watson, Ellen Graf-Martin, Kara Bird, Jennifer Dukes Lee, and Renee Swope. You bring so much joy to my life and add so much goodness to my words. Let's have coffee soon.

To Mama Carmen's Coffee Shop (www.mamacarmen.com)—Thanks for such a great place to write this book. I love your mission and your story and your almond milk lattes.

Most of all, to Jesus—Thank you for the privilege of being part of the work you're doing in this generation. I pray that all I write will bring you glory and delight. Everything we do and all we are is about and for you. Amen.

Notes

Chapter 1 Unexpectedly Fiercehearted

1. Genesis 4:1 KJV.
2. See Psalm 4:4 NLT.

Chapter 2 Being Woman

1. Sharon Jaynes, *How Jesus Broke the Rules to Set You Free: God's Plan for Women to Walk in Power and Purpose* (Eugene, OR: Harvest House, 2015), Kindle edition, chap. 1.

Chapter 5 Hiding in Stalls

1. Susan Cain, *Quiet: The Power of Introverts in a World That Can't Stop Talking* (New York: Crown Publishing Group, 2013), Kindle edition, Introduction.
2. Elaine Aron, *The Highly Sensitive Person* (New York: Kensington, 2013), Kindle edition.

Chapter 8 Mango Closet

1. Kaitlyn E. Bouchillon, *Even If Not: Living, Loving, and Learning in the in Between* (CreateSpace Independent Publishing Platform, 2016), 3.

Chapter 14 Praying Wronger

1. Matthew 6:10 KJV.

Chapter 19 Like Water into Wine

1. Ed Stetzer, "The Real Reason Young Adults Drop Out of Church," ChristianityToday.com, December 1, 2014, http://www.christianitytoday.com/edstetzer/2014/december/real-reasons-young-adults-drop-out-of-church.html.

Chapter 21 Crazy Sparks

1. Gretchen Rubin, *Better Than Before: What I Learned about Making and Breaking Habits—to Sleep More, Quit Sugar, Procrastinate Less, and Generally Build a Happier Life* (New York: Broadway Books, 2015), Kindle edition, chap. 1.

Chapter 22 Ordinary, Divine

1. Emily P. Freeman, *Simply Tuesday: Small Moment Living in a Fast-Moving World* (Grand Rapids: Revell, 2015), 119–20.

2. "Brother Lawrence: Practitioner of God's Presence," *Christianity Today*, accessed April 13, 2017, http://www.christianitytoday.com/history/people/inner travelers/brother-lawrence.html.

3. "Westminster Shorter Catechism Project," ShorterCatechism.com, accessed April 12, 2017, http://www.shortercatechism.com/resources/wsc/wsc _001.html.

Chapter 23 All Favorites

1. Romans 2:11.

Chapter 27 Pedicures, Mice, Therapy

1. Henry Cloud, *The Power of the Other* (New York: HarperBusiness, 2016), Kindle edition, chap. 2.

Chapter 28 Brave, Hard Thing

1. Jennifer Dukes Lee, *The Happiness Dare: Pursuing Your Heart's Deepest, Holiest, and Most Vulnerable Desire* (Carol Stream, IL: Tyndale, 2016), Kindle edition, chap. 6.

Chapter 31 On Ragamuffins

1. *Ragamuffin*, directed by David Leo Schultz (Los Angeles: Color Green Films, 2013).

Chapter 32 Kind, Not Nice

1. Harriet Braiker, *The Disease to Please: Curing the People-Pleasing Syndrome* (New York: McGraw-Hill, 2006), Kindle edition.

2. R. J. Palacio, *Wonder* (New York: Random House, 2012), Kindle edition.

Chapter 35 Not the Only One

1. C. S. Lewis, *The Four Loves* (San Diego: Harcourt Brace International, 1991), 65.

Chapter 36 Hey There, Friend

1. Maria Konnikova, "The Limits of Friendship," *The New Yorker*, October 8, 2014, www.newyorker.com/science/maria-konnikova/social-media-affect -math-dunbar-number-friendships.

Chapter 37 Farther, Not Faster

1. Eugene Peterson, *A Long Obedience in the Same Direction: Discipleship in an Instant Society*, 2nd ed. (Downers Grove, IL: InterVarsity, 2000), 17.

Holley Gerth wishes she could have coffee with you. And if she could, she'd never mention any of this, because she'd be too busy listening to you and loving it.

Holley is the *Wall Street Journal* bestselling author of *You're Already Amazing* as well as several other books. She's also a licensed counselor, certified life coach, and speaker who helps women embrace who they are, become all God created them to be, and live intentionally.

Holley cofounded (in)courage.me, an online destination for women that received almost one million page views in its first six months. She also partners with DaySpring. Her personal site, HolleyGerth.com, serves almost forty thousand subscribers.

Outside the word world, Holley is the wife of Mark, and together they're parents to Lovelle—a daughter they adopted when she was twenty-one years old because God is full of surprises.

Holley is passionate about empowering girls in poverty to become fiercehearted women. Find out more at compassion.com /fiercehearted.

CONNECT WITH

Holley

HOLLEYGERTH.COM
FIERCEHEARTED.COM

@HolleyGerth